And the Angels wept

And the Angels Wept

From the Pulpits of Oklahoma City After the Bombing

Edited by
Marsha Brock Bishop
and David P. Polk

Cover Photo: Roger Bondy
Cover Design: Lynne Condellone
Art Director: Michael Domínguez

10 9 8 7 6 5 4 3 2 1

Library of Congress Cataloging–in–Publication Data
(pending)

Printed in the United States of America

All royalties derived from the sale of *And the Angels Wept* go to the Interfaith Disaster Recovery of Greater Oklahoma City.

The mission of this coalition of seventeen religious groups is to meet the unmet needs of the community during the long-term recovery process, a process which is projected to continue for at least the next two years. A key objective of the group is to bring together the resources within the religious community, thereby making the most efficient use of those recources.

A thirteen-member board of directors has been elected to meet weekly to allocate both human and financial resources. The community-at-large group is also meeting weekly and has formed a number of working committees.

Interfaith Disaster Recovery may be reached at its Oklahoma City office at (405) 524-0338 or through the Oklahoma Conference of Churches office at (405) 525-2928.

Contents

Introduction

Marsha Brock Bishop

The words of a camp song, a round, have haunted me during the days following the bombing—an event that marked the end of a certain innocence and trust held by most of us who live in what has been called the "heartland." It is based on the first verse of Psalm 137:

> By the waters, the waters of Babylon
> We lay down and wept, and wept, for thee, Zion.
> We remember, we remember, we remember thee, Zion.

We have wept, as have many of you—tears of anger, of grief, of compassion, of remembrance, and, finally, tears of hope from the overwhelming outpouring of compassion from people everywhere. And we have been aware of the tears of the One who has strengthened us in our journey and who has walked with us every step of the way, the tears of God.

Gathering the sermons and responses in this small collection has been a labor of love and a tribute to all the people who lost their lives, those who were injured, the families, the rescue workers, and all those who responded to the tragedy in Oklahoma City. Reading the sermons from pastors who preached during those first days following the bombing calls forth again the strong emotions we all felt. These are words from the heart, emotional, struggling to explain and understand that which is possibly beyond understanding. But, most importantly, they are words of faith and hope.

Many of the pastors shared the same response, as they prepared their sermons. So many had preached from hurried notes, trusting that God would guide them as they spoke. They had spent their time giving pastoral care to the people. "Will it be acceptable to piece together my notes? I didn't have time to prepare a manuscript," and, "I'm not sure this sermon is suitable for publication. It's so personal," were remarks I heard again and again. I am grateful to them and to the church secretaries who set aside other things to transcribe some of the messages from audiotape. I am also grateful to my husband, Larry Bishop, whose patience and expertise on the computer saved my nerves repeatedly.

The responses fall into two broad categories: those intended for everyone whose lives were touched by the tragedy, and those intended for members of a specific congregation. Included in the first category are the messages of President Bill Clinton, Dr. Billy Graham, and Governor Frank Keating at the memorial service, "A Time for Healing," held at the State Fair Arena, Sunday, April 23; prayers from the Community Prayer Service, April 20; and the sermons preached at the Family Assistance Center at the First Christian Church by Dr. Earl A. Grollman, a certified grief counselor as well as an ordained rabbi, on April 23, and by Rev. Don Alexander, pastor of the First Christian Church, on April 30. The second category is messages from pastors to their home congregations. There is the first communion message for children at St. John the Baptist Catholic Church from Father John Petusky; a pastoral letter and sermon for Village United Methodist Church from Rev. Tish Malloy; and sermons that relate personal experiences of both pastor and church members from others. The sermons and messages represent Protestant, Catholic, nondenominational Christians, Jewish, Islam, and Baha'i. This has been a time for all people of faith to turn to God.

I suppose each of us will carry images of the bombing, the massive destruction of property, the heartache of bleeding and dying children and adults, with us the rest of our lives. But the days that followed have been amazing ones. A most incredible thing has happened, something that continues even now. And, to me, it is as awe-inspiring as the bomb blast was devastating. I am speaking of goodness.

In a letter to the editor of the *Daily Oklahoman*, Don Alexander, the pastor of First Christian Church in Oklahoma City, wrote, "Tragedy does not produce goodness, but sometimes it can reveal it." In the days following April 19, goodness has been revealed in remarkable depth and dimension.

I know most of you have watched much of this on television, just as I have, but I wish each of you could have personally experienced the tremendous outpouring of love and compassion. I have had the opportunity to be present at First Christian Church as part of a team that notifies families of death. Each time I entered the church, I was amazed again at the sheer numbers of people offering to help.

But it wasn't just at the church, or the bombsite, or the hospitals that help was offered. Everywhere we turned, there was another act of kindness. In the parking lot of Wal Mart, a big charcoal cooker was set up, selling hamburgers for a dollar—to go to the fund to help victims. Restaurants, grocery stores, churches, volunteers prepared mountains of food and delivered it to all the many places people were gathered to help. University students and children gathered supplies and money. Such beautiful expressions of kindness, from the very young to the very old, have been inspiring and, yes, amazing.

Because of them, now we have other images to remember—images of beauty, of love, of generosity of spirit, of courage. And we are reminded that God's love is neverending, boundless—and expressed in the faces and actions of ordinary people who became extraordinary. The words of the apostle Paul to the church at Philippi echo in my heart, "Finally, beloved, whatever is true, whatever is honorable, whatever is just, whatever is pure, whatever is pleasing, whatever is commendable, if there is any excellence and if there is anything worthy of praise, think about these things....And the God of peace will be with you" (Philippians 4:8–9). May it be so for you.

A Message of Hope

Dr. Robert E. Long

Rev. Long *is senior minister of St. Luke's United Methodist Church. Only a few blocks from the explosion, he and his pastoral staff were among the first to arrive at the site to offer pastoral care for survivors who were coming out of the Murrah Building. He offered the church as a center for the Red Cross, the blood bank, and for victims and families who needed an immediate place to gather following the disaster.*

Psalm 46

Where were you when you heard the news that the Japanese had bombed Pearl Harbor? It was over fifty years ago, but if you were alive, I bet you remember exactly. Where were you when you heard that John F. Kennedy had been shot and killed in Dallas? Where were you when you heard that the Challenger space shuttle had exploded and all the astronauts were dead? Where were you last Wednesday a little after 9:00 in the morning when you felt the explosion, or you heard the news? I bet as long as you live you will never forget—nor would you want to—because the events of the last week have touched all of our lives so very deeply. The events of the last week have touched our nation, and we will never be exactly the same.

I was down here at the office. It was in the morning, and I was sitting at my desk—we're only ten blocks away—when the explosion happened, and it rocked this building. There was mortar in my brick wall that literally came tumbling out. It shook the place so violently, and yet amazingly only one window in our building was broken. But I think I just naturally hollered out—it was such a shock—and I jumped out of my chair and went running out into the office area. I was hollering, "What's happened?" I was hollering for staff. What I thought had happened was the boiler in the basement must have exploded. We went running toward the basement when somebody else said, "No, it's a building downtown."

We stepped outside, and we saw the smoke rising, and already we could hear the sirens. We didn't go running downtown; we knew there would be many people there. The emergency medical people needed to get there, the police would be there, so we came back inside. We talked for a moment, and then we called the Red Cross to say, we want to offer our facilities if you need it, if we can help. Then we called to say, if you need to set up a blood center, you can do that here. We're all participating in blood donation activities of sharing blood. Then I called down to First Methodist Church, which is about a block away from the explosion, to say, if you have children in your child-care center and need a place for them, we will bring them up here. If you need to come, whatever we can do, we are happy to help you. It was only an hour or two later that we got a call from Robert Allen, the pastor at Wesley United Methodist Church. He was downtown arranging for chaplains for survivors who were coming out of the building, and he asked if we would come. So Rev. Dave Poteet and I went hurrying downtown.

Since we were so close, we were two of the very first to get there. We were standing around waiting for everyone to get organized when we began to see the different survivors coming out. We started talking to them. We would come back up here and we would talk to survivors and people who had lost loved ones. We would talk to some of those who had been displaced from their homes. I have been talking with you in the serving line, helping to prepare food. And during these last days that we've all gotten together to talk, I've been hearing some of the same things over and over again, by all different kinds of people. We all seem to have the same questions and the same statements, and we've all been talking. What I want to do this morning is to share some things I've been hearing that keep coming up over and over again. I think it's important that we come together as a family and talk about it today. I want to share with you four things I keep hearing.

First of all, I keep hearing everybody ask: "Why?" Why did it happen to me? Why Oklahoma City? Why? When I talk to people who have survived, they say, "Why me?" When I talk to people who have lost love ones, they ask, "Why?" When Dave and I got downtown, we were some of those first ones there, and as we were standing around, we saw two ladies. They looked rather shocked, disoriented. No one really was there with them, so we went over to speak to them. Dave was speaking to one lady and I was speaking to the other, and the lady just wanted to talk. She said, "I was in the building on the seventh floor." She said, "I was sitting there at my desk talking to a friend, and suddenly my desk went down...and they were gone. Why me?"

My son Paul has a schoolmate. She just came here two weeks ago. The family is still living in a hotel, they haven't had time to get a house yet. You see, the father got a promotion—a transfer—here to Oklahoma City and went to work in the building...and now he is missing. Two weeks ago—and now he is gone.

I saw two ladies outside my office in the narthex, and I could tell—I could see it in their eyes—they were friends; both of their husbands worked together. I was out there talking to them and one of them said her husband had been gone and was not in the building. The other husband had been at work that day, and he was missing. Why one? Why not the other?

Yesterday, I was in our Christian Life Center talking to a lady who had come up from New Mexico. You see, her brother had been up here, and he had gone to the building at 9:00 that morning to get his Social Security card. He had been there four minutes...and they can't find him. I know another man who has been in the military working in that building for years, and he retired a month ago. But more than twenty of his colleagues and the person who took his desk...they're gone. And everybody seems to ask—Why? Why me?

When I heard that question over and over again, I couldn't help but think about Arthur Ashe. Arthur Ashe is the greatest African-American tennis player our country has ever produced. He wrote a book entitled *Days of Grace.* He tells how he had open-heart surgery—bypass surgery—and was given tainted blood, from which he developed AIDS. In that book Arthur Ashe says, "When I discovered that I had AIDS, I didn't ask 'Why me?' because when I won Wimbledon and the U. S. Open, I didn't ask 'Why me?' No, I asked the question, 'Why not me?'" Why not me? Why must it always be somebody else? Good or bad.

One of the things I do not believe is that it was God's will that anybody die in that building last Wednesday. I don't believe it was all those people's time. I don't believe that God wanted those people to die. No, I think it reminds us that we live in a free world, that God has created us and set us free, and in our freedom we can choose to hate and hurt and destroy, and in our freedom, we can choose to love and build up and heal. When we read our scripture lesson this morning, we were reading about the city of Zion that has known warfare and pain and hurt. It happens in the Holy Land; it happens everywhere. The question is not "Why me?" but "Why not me?" because the truth is, bad things do happen to good people. That's a part of it. Why not me?

Second, I have heard so many people saying, "God was with me. I'm alive, I survived. God was with me."

To all those people, I say, "You're right. God was with you, and we're so grateful you're alive." But I also want to say this morning that I believe God was with all those people who died too. That's the message of Easter—God is with us when we live, and God is with us when we die. And I believe that when those people were coming to face that moment of death, God was there for them to give them resurrection and new life. It's not that God loved one better than another. God is with us in life, and God is with us in death. I believe God is with those families who lost somebody they love, so that in the midst of this grief when their hearts are breaking, there is a spirit of hope to go on. Again, our scripture says so very much: "God is a very present help in trouble." In those hard times, yes, God is with us, and for those who lived, let us give thanks, and for those who died, let us celebrate the message of Easter, and for those who are without a loved one, let us pray they find strength, for the good news is God is with us all, and that's why we have hope and we go on today—because our faith says God is with us.

Third, so many people have been saying, "Oklahoma City? If it happened in Oklahoma City, it can happen anywhere! I don't feel safe! Where can I run? I am afraid. If it happens here in Oklahoma City, it can happen in Boise, Idaho; Des Moines, Iowa; Springfield, Illinois; or Biloxi, Mississippi. It can happen anywhere. How can I be safe?"

Three months ago I told you how I lost a very special friend, Scott DeBerry. He was thirty-five years old; he was a private pilot, and he was killed in a plane crash. A father of three children, a husband. I too am a private pilot, and I'm building my own airplane that I intend to fly. After the crash happened, I had to admit, I had to stop and think, "Am I being crazy? Am I tempting fate pursuing this dream? Am I getting out here doing something stupid?"

But then this week comes along and I think of all these people who were sitting in downtown Oklahoma City at their desks, and they too are gone. I am reminded that it doesn't matter whether you're flying in a homebuilt airplane or whether you're sitting at your desk, you're not safe. You see, the truth of the matter is, we are all going to die someday, and I don't know when that will happen for me or for you. The issue is, we're not called to live in fear of dying, we are called to live with confidence today. And I believe that this event simply reminds us that today is the day we are given and tomorrow is promised to no one. Don't go running in fear. Don't go running looking for safety. The call is to live today in confidence. "Therefore, we will not fear though the earth should change," for God is with us. You can't run and hide. There is nowhere to be safe. Don't live in fear. The call is to live today with meaning and purpose and joy, for tomorrow is promised to no one.

There is that old saying, "If you knew you were going to die, if you knew you had a very short time to live, whom would you call? What would you say? Why are you waiting?" Tomorrow is promised to no one. The call is to live today confidently, because we walk with our Christ.

Fourth, over and over again I've heard so many people say, "I'm angry. I'm mad. This was wrong—what happened?" If you watched on the news, then you saw a prisoner being brought out in Perry, Oklahoma, and you heard the anger. I believe that's a perfectly acceptable response—to be angry. We need to be angry whenever we see innocent people being killed and hurt. We need to stand up and speak out against white supremacist groups, or terrorists, or people who are going out and killing abortionists, doctors, anyone who is killing and hurting other people—we need to get angry and speak out. But I also know that if we let our anger turn into hate, then we are no better than those who have hated and hurt us. Easter tells us that hate is not the final word, that hate does not have to be the response to hate. There is another way.

What I'd like to suggest is that maybe, just maybe, we use our anger as the energy that leads us into acts of love and healing. Anger is energy, and let our anger be the energy that spurs us on to acts of love and healing and kindness and wholeness. That's the proper response of anger. You know, we can't change the whole world. I can't stop all the white supremacist groups. I can't stop all the terrorist groups, and neither can you. We can't stop all the hate, but you know, we can do something.

In my article this week in the paper, I quoted Edward Everett Hale who said, "I am only one, but still I am one. I cannot do everything, but still I can do something. And because I cannot do everything, I will not refuse to do something that I can do." You can do something, and this week so many of you have been doing something. I want to tell you that I'm proud to be an Oklahoman this week, and I'm proud to be a part of this church because I've seen the way that you and the entire city have responded.

On that first night when we opened the shelter, so many companies here in Oklahoma City began bringing in food. It was not requested, no one asked; they just brought it. We could have fed a thousand people here. We were feeding volunteers working downtown, feeding at the shelter, so many people. I have seen so many of you at the doors to greet and to direct. You've been answering the phones, working on computers; you've been there cooking in the kitchen, serving in the lines. You've been there sorting clothes. You've been there to care. No, we cannot change the whole world, but you know we can do something, and you've been doing it; and that is so good, because that's the way we make a difference. We take our anger and we turn it into actions of love and change the world.

Let me tell you something else. As you begin offering your love and doing those things, not only are you going to help somebody else. I've discovered it helps you with your own grief. It's when you decide that you are going to offer those acts of love that you not only help somebody else, you help yourself. You help yourself in your grieving time.

As I said earlier, we had a number of people in our Christian Life Center who had been left without their homes, without clothes, without money. They can't go back, they won't be let in right now. I've been going through there, getting to know some of the people. One evening recently I was walking through the Christian Life Center, and I saw one of these men coming the other way and I happened to look at him, and I thought, *you know, I've got a shirt that looks just like that.* A few moments later another person came by and I thought, *I've got a shirt that looks like that.* It was a few minutes later that my wife came up to me and said, "You know, Bob, there are some nice men here who can't get back in and get their clothes. I hope you don't mind. I went home and got some of your clothes to give to them."

Next time I saw them come by, I thought, *you know, they really look good.* But I also felt so good, because when you see somebody in need and you're able to share, not only do you help them but it does something to help you. It is true that bad things happen to good people. Why not me? But God is with us, whether we're living or dying. God is with us, so we don't have to be afraid and run looking for safety. We live today confidently, and in that spirit of love, we begin to reach out and share, and that's how you change the world.

I know that President Clinton has said that today is a national day of mourning, but I wish he would have also added that today is a national day of mourning and of hope and of new beginnings, because God is with us, and love is not defeated. "God is our refuge and strength, a very present help in trouble. Therefore we will not fear."

It's in the name of the Father, and the Son, and the Holy Spirit. Amen.

Easter's Been Disrupted!

J. Pat Kennedy

Rev. Kennedy *is pastor of St. Andrews Presbyterian Church in Oklahoma City. He is Disaster Response Coordinator for Indian Nations Prebytery.*

Psalm 46:1–7; Acts 5:27–32

The house shook, the windows rattled, the shelf fell, and antique pictures and pots broke on the floor. Outside I saw white smoke in the distance floating over houses. Neighbors came out and we all asked, "What was that?" We had no answers. My neighbor, Eric, said his windows were broken. I checked mine, and turned on the TV and there it was. The Federal Office Building had been bombed.

Bombed out! Half of it was gone! An act of terrorism fifteen blocks from my home. The worst in American history.

Among all the thoughts and feelings that I've had, ranging from sadness to anger to frustration to helplessness and powerlessness, the one that comes crashing into my consciousness this morning is: "Easter's been disrupted." Easter's been disrupted.

This morning you and I are gathered here to give thanks for life, and to praise almighty God who is the giver of life. We do this not because we want to but because our faith demands it of us. That's why we're here in this church, in this place where the main activity is the worship of God, the Father of our Lord Jesus Christ, the God and Father of us all. But as we say this, our hearts are heavy with the pain and grief we share as we face the headlines in the local and national newspapers. We've all felt the untimely deaths and tragedy in our city. There is something that rises up in us and says, "It can't be. It shouldn't have happened. It's not right. It makes no sense."

We are left with that awful haunting question. "Why?" Why did this happen? Again and again, why? It reminded me of one of my favorite books by Nikos Kazantzakis, who wrote *Zorba the Greek*. In this book Zorba is a Greek man who has lost his son in death. He has been trying to find a way of coping with his son's death, and he has cried and shrieked and yelled and cursed and even danced. And he turns to his boss and says, "Why do the young die? Why do the young have to die? Why does anyone have to die?" And his boss says back, "I don't know. I don't know." And Zorba says in his anger, in his rage at the death and the loss of his son, "Well, what's the use of all your books then? If they don't tell you that, what do they tell you?" And the boss says back, "They tell me of the agony of people who can't answer questions like yours."

In these few moments, what will we do with our "why"? For one thing, I believe that we can state according to the scriptures that death is not the will of God. The scriptures are pretty clear on this. In John's Gospel, Jesus states that he has come from God that we, God's children, might have life and have it abundantly. That's one thing we know for sure about God's will, that God gives us life and wants us to enjoy it to the full. In the passage that we read in Paul's letter to the Corinthians, "the last enemy to be destroyed is death." It seems clear throughout the New Testament that death is the interrupter, always interrupting what God has given—life. Death stalks us, which is why we are here today: to affirm life and the Giver of life.

This means that we will not pretend that anyone's death is the will of God. We will not say that God needed or wanted anyone to be with God in heaven. For God is already with us wherever we are here on earth, and God is with us out of love, not out of need. So let us not say or think that death is something God arranges for us, for death is not God's will.

But having said that, what can we say about what is God's will? We've already affirmed that God wants us to have life, abundant life—so much that God freely gives us this life here on earth and then sends us Jesus to give us another kind of life: eternal life, a new order of things, a new creation. And we have gotten a glimpse of that resurrection life in Jesus. New life may begin here and now. When this mortal life ends, as Paul says, death will be "swallowed up in victory," the victory that is assured us by the risen Lord. That is God's will for us. The whole New Testament proclaims this eternal life in God, in the new creation; and in this present life we already enjoy a God-given freedom to live life.

But so often in our lives the question "Why?" doesn't get answered. Nor should we force an answer in our effort to know why. For us to insist that there must be answers leads us to make a monster out of the real question for us here this morning. The real question for us is not "Why?" but "How?" Now that this has happened, *how* will we face it? How may we find the strength to face our pain and grief and go on affirming life and the God who gives us that life? God does not protect us from pain or from life's tragic shocks. Rather, God meets us in the midst of it, and here we are today as God has always met us—with love that dies on a cross and then rises to meet us again. And only in that faith and hope can we keep going. That's why we've come here today to share our faith and our hope even in the midst of our tears and our unanswered questions.

It is instructive for us in the Gospel lesson that was not read this morning, in Jesus' appearance to the disciples at Emmaus and the appearance to Thomas, that his last words to his disciples before ascending to the Father were these: "Fear not, bear witness, receive power" (paraphrasing Luke 24:38 and Acts 1:8). And so Peter, in The Acts of the Apostles lesson this morning, is in Jerusalem preaching the Easter message that Christ is risen, and he is being confronted by those in authority to stop preaching, but he says, "We are witnesses to these things." They knew in a way that is difficult to understand for people who don't know, because death keeps trying to break back in on the Easter message—the resurrection of life, and life eternal—and it will not have its way.

Peter's message in the heart of Jerusalem is that death cannot undo what was done at Easter—that Christ is risen and that we live in the hope of the resurrection and that Easter cannot be undone by death, so that there is nothing in all creation that will separate us from the love of God. And so in Corinthians Paul reminds us, as he reminds his readers, to remember that "Christ died for our sins in accordance with the scriptures, and that he was buried, and that he was raised on the third day." Remembering is crucial because Christian hope is based on the resurrection. "If Christ has not been raised...we are of all people most to be pitied," Paul says, because our hope will turn out to have been a delusion. Better not to have hoped at all than to have hope dashed. But what is hope?

Hope is not the same as optimism. Optimism is based on assumptions that things are going well. Optimism assumes that the good things will continue and bring positive results. Hope does not arise from an idea that we will always be successful in life or that life will always give us good things. Hope can be present amid the worst kind of gloom. Hope arises not from the event itself but from something outside the situation. It is a dim light gleaming through the darkness. Hope is based not on what I can do, but on what God has done and is doing.

There are times in our lives when an evaluation of what's going on, a careful look at our situation, gives us little hope. But unlike optimism, hope comes from outside the situation. Jesus did not raise himself from the dead. Jesus was raised from the dead. Easter gives us hope because it promises that God will do for believers what God has done for Jesus. We must have confidence that a power is at work outside ourselves if we are to sustain hope amid the gloom and doom of our lives.

If the Easter message were the end of the struggle, its message would promise immunity from the evil of this world. But we are not promised immunity from the evil of this world. We are promised hope in the Easter message. Christ's resurrection is the foundation of our hope. So in the meantime—and times like this are indeed "mean times"—we live with hope.

We immerse ourselves in the struggle to undo the patterns of evil, terror, death, and destruction. Hope gives us the capacity to struggle even when there is no end in sight. And so how do we deal with the call that Jesus gave to his disciples when they were most in fear after his death? "Fear not, bear witness, receive power!"

Well, I've seen God's people all over town this week. I've seen the grace of God in people's lives even in the midst of death and destruction: giving food to the hungry, digging through rubble, rescuing the injured, comforting people, sorting and helping distribute mountains of clothing. Hospital staffs working to save lives. People caring for young children while parents went through the process of seeking help and relief. Touching and holding, hugging in yards, bagging food items. Serving meals to weary, scared, and bone-tired people. Giving comfort to those who lost loved ones. Carrying on one's duties but with the additional added duty of helping where one can, cheerfully and willingly.

I saw the people of God gather together in the ministry of helping others, not only in worship services, but in streets and on sidewalks and in family groups of two or three. Sobbing for those who hurt and feeling the pain of loss. I saw the grace of God coming to people across phone lines throughout this nation from near and far. And we did ask the questions, "Why?" and "How much can we take?" "How much more?" And yet knowing that God is big enough for all the questions that our hearts can ask, we gather as true believers, a fellowship of believers not dependent on buildings or the membership of churches, but together as a community—God's people. I've seen, this week, God's people at work being the people who are called to be in the places where God can use us. And I offer thanks for the privilege of being part of the people of God and this community in this time.

Martin Luther, one of the outstanding figures in the history of the Protestant church, served his fellow Christians in no greater way than in writing and composing one of the world's best loved hymns, "A Mighty Fortress Is Our God." It was written in the late summer of 1529 when the famed German theologian, after a long period of deep depression, had found spiritual comfort in the strength of Psalm 46. He repeated over and over these words: "God is our refuge and strength, God is our refuge and strength, a very present help in times of trouble." And with this thought in mind, he hurled his defiance at all his foes, physical and spiritual—all his struggles of mind and body, the opposition of people—and penned the words never forgotten by the Christian church:

> A mighty fortress is our God,
> a bulwark never failing.

Our helper he amid the flood
of mortal ills prevailing.
For still our ancient foe
doth seek to work us woe,
his craft and power are great
and armed with cruel hate,
on earth is not his equal.

Our scripture today, in the psalm and in Acts, tells us there is a power let loose in this world, a power that rises from the grave, a power for good that cannot be contained by principalities or powers. Nothing can separate us from the love of God. God has raised Jesus from the dead, and we need not be amazed that death is destructive because Easter can be a threat to this world, a world that often prefers darkness over light and death over life.

The story of salvation asks each of us, "Where are we in this story?" And those hoping finally to put a once-and-for-all end to this Jesus commotion—this death breaking in on Easter, disrupting Easter—find that our voice will be out there in the streets and in the sanctuaries and in our neighborhoods and with our friends and with people we don't even know: the poor, the dispossessed, the rich, all kinds of people praising God for God's work in Jesus Christ and being witnesses because they've heard: "Fear not, bear witness, receive power."

So where do we see ourselves today is in the midst of this Easter disruption? "God is our refuge and our strength, our present help in trouble."

God's Face Is Toward Us

Lura J. Cayton

Rev. Cayton *is pastor of Capitol Hill Christian Church, which is located very near the downtown area. She serves as treasurer of Interfaith Disaster Recovery of Greater Oklahoma City.*

Romans 8:18–39

What a difference a week makes! It seems an eternity since we gathered to sing and dance and celebrate God's great victory over death in the resurrection of Jesus Christ. Some weeks go by without anything happening that we will remember over a long period of time. But how many of us will forget where we were and what we were doing Wednesday, April 19, 1995, at 9:02 a.m.? Our hearts and our lives changed in that instant.

After the initial wondering about what the sound was and feeling the earth shake, images began to invade our consciousness. Images that we are used to glancing at on the evening news. Images that most often are not very real for us. They appear on the screen and then they disappear. But this was not

Bosnia. This was not Rwanda. This was not Beirut. And as we remained glued to our TV screens for nearly twenty-four hours a day, the images and the stories kept coming. This was Oklahoma City, our home, and the images would not disappear. And our hearts are broken. Our minds are confused. Our emotions are spent. And our souls are troubled.

One of the ways to deal with these emotions associated with our grief is to talk about them, to tell our stories. What happened to you? What are your concerns over friends or acquaintances, those who have experienced losses, those who have volunteered?

My stories begin with a phone call from Pam very shortly after the blast. Pam worked for a company with offices in the Journal Record Building. When the ceiling began to fall she left her purse, her coat, and everything else to escape the building. She was physically uninjured but scared to death. She wanted to know if, since she had no family to go home to, it would be all right to come to the church for a while. We were able to talk about her experience and watch events unfold on the TV. Then I took her to her rooming house to secure another key to her room.

About 4 o'clock I decided to go to the southside blood bank to see how long the line was. It was a six-hour wait so I returned at 10 p.m. and had the dubious distinction of being the last donor out the door at 1:30 a.m. In line ahead of me were three women who were obviously there together. One of them was a military veteran. When she finally reached the point of the final screening, she was told she could not donate because she had had surgery too recently. She was crushed. It was extremely important to her to be able to share her life's blood with someone else. Instead she ended up running the vacuum over the donation center carpet while she waited for her friends.

(At this point I moved down into the congregation and invited anyone who would like to share stories to do so. Many mentioned the names of friends and relatives who were still missing and their families and the waiting, or friends and relatives who were fire-

fighters involved in the rescue attempts or volunteer chaplains and caregivers and Red Cross workers serving in different ways. One told of her experience serving meals and snacks to personnel at the medical examiner's headquarters. Thanksgiving was expressed for First Christian Church's willingness to open their doors to the families who were waiting. Another shared about how The Guardian Funeral Home on his mail route had received instructions from national headquarters that there was to be no charge for services for infants in the day-care center. Another shared how she had been in the HUD office the day before but it could just as well have been Wednesday. One of the people she worked with most frequently had gone to the bathroom and had walked out alive, but five others that she worked closely with were still missing.)

We could continue to tell stories and we will continue to tell stories. As we do so, we will be aware of the different stages of the journey through grief. We are aware of the numbness we have felt and the disbelief. There are expressed emotions. Tears have poured from our eyes. Some have expressed fear that the same thing might happen again and to them. Anger has been directed at anyone who could do such a thing, and why didn't they take better care of the children and why wasn't there more security? Surely somebody saw someone running from that truck; why didn't they call authorities? There is anger at the loss of children and pain at seeing them in such pain.

Children have been experiencing insecurity, nightmares, and the loss of innocence. They have no framework for understanding what has happened. There is grief over the loss of parents and grandparents and aunts and uncles and cousins.

In some cases there is a sense of isolation, an aloneness almost as if each of us were going through this alone. We are drawn to the TV screen and to the scene and the waiting is interminable.

There will be depression and questioning. Why? Why? Why? Why would anyone do such a thing? And blame. It would be much easier had it been a natural disaster or if there had been a gasoline explosion, or if we could blame someone from the outside, some foreigner. But how could it be one of us? We don't kill children and innocent people. We try to make sense out of what seems to us a senseless act. And why in Oklahoma City? Those things happen in Los Angeles or New York City. But this is our home.

There is guilt. Could we be doing more to respond? Why wasn't it me? How have we created a climate in which this could happen?

But gradually there will be a return to reality. We are left not knowing what to do. It is a feeling that leaves us sick to our stomachs. We want to make it better, to kiss the wound and put a Band-Aid on it. We hope against hope that somehow more people will be found alive, especially the children.

It will take time for us to deal with these emotions and to journey through grief. Healing does come. It comes as we offer love and support to each other. For some of us, it comes as we become more aware of the facts and how it happened. Healing comes as we become aware of the stories and families remember their loved ones. But most of all healing comes through our faith.

For me the passage we read from Romans 8:18–39 is one of the most helpful. It is a passage of hope, a passage that affirms that nothing in life can separate us from the love of God. We are never outside God's loving care. God is always present with us.

That doesn't keep us from wondering how or why such things could happen. But those are questions for which we do not always have answers. But we can let our sorrow and grief work for us. Think about it. The disaster was caused by the specific actions of a very few individuals. Yet look at the hundreds of thousands that it has brought together. People who bring expertise to help and people who are just concerned, people who have to respond in some way to work through their grief.

Friends and family members have called to express concern about our well-being and that of our congregation. Individuals have done things that they never in this world dreamed they would need to do or could do.

Harry Emerson Fosdick wrote about what a strange paradox our life is! We dread tragedy and yet there is nothing on earth that we admire more than a person who handles it triumphantly. Much as we deplore the hardships and troubles that Lincoln suffered, we know that his quality of character never could have come from ease, comfort, and pleasantness alone. He did not simply endure his tragedies; he built character out of them. Trouble and grief can add a new dimension to life. Some people's lives end in defeat and collapse. Others, thank God, can say with Paul: we triumph even in our troubles.

The Christian response can be found in the events that we have experienced through Lent and Easter: the tragic death of Jesus on the cross, which represents our relationship to God but also represents our relationship to each other. Even in the midst of the tragedy of Jesus' death he reached out to those who hung on either side of him. The hope of the resurrection is not only that death is conquered, but that it is a point of transformation. That God is present at death as God is present in all life makes it possible for us to journey through sorrow and pain.

A young man's wife died, leaving him with a small son. After returning from the cemetery, they went to bed as soon as it was dark, because there was nothing else the father could bear to do. As he lay there in the darkness—brokenhearted, grief-stricken, numb with sorrow—the boy broke the stillness from his little bed with a disturbing question: "Daddy, where is Mommy?"

The father tried to get the boy to go to sleep, but the questions kept coming from his confused, childish mind. After a while, the father got up and brought the boy to bed with him.

But the child was still disturbed and restless, and occasionally would ask a probing, heart-rending question.

Finally, the boy reached out in the darkness and placed his hand on his father's face asking, "Daddy, is your face toward me?"

Assured by his father's words, and by his own touch, that his father's face was indeed toward him, the boy said, "If your face is toward me, I think I can go to sleep." And in a little while, he was quiet.[1]

The proclamation of our Christian faith is that God has not rejected us, but that in raising Jesus Christ from the dead, God's face is toward us. We may not see the end. We may not see the light. We may not understand the "whys." But we don't have to. God has heard our cries. God knows our sorrow and grief and pain. But the tears will be wiped away. For nothing can separate us—life or death—from the love of God. God's face is toward us.

[1] James W. Moore, *When Grief Breaks Your Heart* (Nashville: Abingdon Press, 1995), pp 9-10.

What Do We Do with Our Pain?

Dr. Earl A. Grollman

Dr. Grollman is a pioneer in the field of crisis intervention. Rabbi Grollman came immediately to Oklahoma City from his home in Massachusetts to assist in grief counseling and training. He has written twenty-one books on the subject, received many humanitarian awards, and hosts a weekly cable television program, "Matters of Life and Death." He spoke at the First Christian Church where victims, families, and volunteers at the Family Assistance Center had joined the congregation that first Sunday after the bombing.

"Jacob...came to a certain place and stayed there for the night....Taking one of the stones of the place, he put it under his head and lay down in that place. And he dreamed that there was a ladder set up on the earth, the top of it reaching to heaven; and the angels of God were ascending and descending on it. And the LORD stood beside him and said, 'I am the LORD, the God of Abraham your father and the God of Isaac....Know that I am with you and will keep you wherever you go'....Then Jacob woke from his sleep and said, 'Surely the LORD is in this place'....And he took the stone that he had put under his head and set it up for a pillar....He called that place Bethel [the House of God]" (Genesis 28:10–19).

And I want you all to know that this rabbi today is in the house of God. I feel that I am in God's house, the *Bethel*, for different reasons. For when I heard the news, I was speaking at a hospital and I turned on the TV to CNN and saw the First Christian Church, a place of support and caring. And in this service today, I feel that same support and love. After the carnage, many people will find God differently, but all of us will be with the same God, the God of love. It is a theme of this service. Some would say the words in Hebrew, some in Latin, some in English, but the words are the same. This is the leitmotif of this service: "The Lord is my shepherd. I shall not want."

I thought of the words of an old rabbi who asked his student, "Do you love me?" The student replied, "Of course, I love you." Then the old rabbi asked, "Do you know what gives me pain?" The student replied, "How could I know what gives you pain?" and the rabbi replied, "If you do not know what gives me pain, you cannot really love me."

Even a thousand miles away, in Boston, where I live, people saw the devastation and were touched and shared the pain, because one touch of sorrow makes the whole world bend and even those who live a thousand miles away feel the pain. The day before I came, I was speaking at Harvard Medical School when the news of the tragedy came. I've never witnessed such apprehension, even about where people would park their cars. We have lost our innocence. The world has changed.

And the question comes about, with the many losses that are occurring: what can we do? When I witnessed the site yesterday, all I could think of was a quotation from the saddest book in the Bible. It's called the book of Lamentations. This is the occasion when the Jews were exiled from their homeland. The first temple was destroyed. And thus the city sits solitary that was so filled with people. These were more than just words from the scripture. This was the vision that I saw not far from here in Oklahoma City.

What do we do with our pain? What do we do with our grief? We need to understand that grief is an emotion, not a disease. Grief is as natural as eating when you're hungry, drinking when you're thirsty, sleeping when you're tired. Grief is nature's way of healing a broken heart. I feel this pain, this anguish, because grief is love not wanting to let go.

What do we do? We have to understand that everyone will grieve differently. Grief is like snowflakes and fingerprints. What is our relationship to the people? How do we handle other kinds of stress in our life? Do we belong to a place like First Christian? What kind of support do we receive? Like this magnificent support that you are receiving.

As I have been watching television this last day and a half in Oklahoma City, I think the real problem is that people will ask, "Well, what are some of the feelings?" and expect an answer. How can we say? Everyone grieves differently. Some people may even think they are losing their mind. "I don't know what's wrong with me. Since my loved one is missing, since my loved one has died, I can't eat. I can't sleep. I can't concentrate. I'm driving my car and I come to a red light and I can't remember if it means stop or go. You know, I even forgot my own name. Am I losing my mind?"

In psychiatry there is a term called "the crazies." You're not losing your mind. When someone is missing, part of you is missing. When someone has died, part of you has died. If it's the death of a child, it's the death of your future. If it's the death of a parent, it's the death of your past. If it's the death of a spouse, it's the death of the present. And for all of us, it's the loss of our innocence.

So what do we do? It's like going to a physician and saying, "I don't feel well." And the physician will say, "Earl, here's a prescription and if you take it, these are some of the effects that you may experience." It doesn't mean that you are going to feel this way, but if you do, these are the natural feelings. Your throat may be dry. You may be tired. You may be sleepy. I think it's important to know as this is occurring.

I've been watching as a spectator. And I think all of us are numb. It's like watching a drama unfold in our own city. We don't believe it. It's a nightmare. When we wake up, we'll find out it didn't really happen. And this is the problem.

Last night when I spoke at the Baptist Hospital, I showed a film I had made of bereaved people. Do you know what the word *bereaved* means? Robbed. I asked this question some years ago. How long do you think grief endures? And all these people had experienced the death of a loved one. Most people said it would be one or two weeks.

And this is my fear. After the President, after Pastor Graham have come, after all the bodies have been recovered, we must know that in all the studies, for many of us the height of depression will come many months later. The tumult and the shouting dies. The captains and the kings depart. The people who were around aren't around any longer. Friends don't know what's wrong with you.

Grief is like a wound. It may not be as red as it had been, but it's there. Every day, an anniversary, Easter—which was just celebrated—when you're driving your car and you hear a certain song, and tears come down from your eyes. It's important for the congregation to know that our love continues beyond the moment when the flowers have withered.

The feelings some of us will have may even include feelings of guilt, because we're children. When we're good, as children,we are rewarded. When we are bad, we are punished. So we say, "What did I do wrong?" How many times have you heard someone ask, after a terrible loss, "Why am I being punished?" as if death is a kind of divine chastisement.

All of us say things we shouldn't say—all of us. All of us may do things at times that we shouldn't do. I think we have to say to people, "I cannot stop you from suffering, but I can stop you from suffering for the wrong reasons." And whatever our faith, we all say God forgives. And each one of us must forgive ourselves and accept our grief, for grief is love not wanting to let go.

And we need to express our feelings. When the pastor mentioned anger a moment ago, I understood. Angry thoughts do not make angry people. Angry thoughts make very human people. We're angry about acts of inhumanity against the innocent. There is a feeling of wrath that some people may feel even against God. And I have come all the way from Harvard to tell you that God can take it!

Abraham yelled at God, "Shall not the God of justice do justly?" Job said, "Cursed be the day that I was born!" And in the New Testament, Jesus said, "My God! My God! Why have you forsaken me?" It's all right to feel many kinds of feelings as long as we don't hurt ourselves or others.

And sometimes, some of us may need to cry. Tears are a tender tribute of yearning. This is the problem. Men and women often grieve differently. I know, for as I was growing up in Baltimore and I fell off of a swing, my parents said, "Earl, big boys don't cry." Men cry in two places: in the movies, because it's dark, and at sporting events. That's manly. Unfortunately, only one out of seven males has a person with whom he will share his innermost thoughts. We talk about business. We talk about sports. We don't talk about these things.

And so, if a child dies, a friend may come to the hospital and ask, "How is your wife doing?" not, "How are you?" You men need to grieve, appropriately and in your own way. Abraham came to bury his wife Sarah and he cried for her. The shortest sentence in the New Testament—what is it? "Jesus wept." We need to cry. We need friends. And we need support, not only at the time of loss, but in the days and years to come. To find the right support system means we need friends who understand where we are, understand our need to commemorate our feelings.

This is the First Christian Church and I'm a rabbi. As clergy we do the same things. When a person is born, we can explain it biologically. We have a service. Some may call it baptism, some may call it circumcision, but we have a service. We make mountains out of moments. We mark when we go through puberty—some call it confirmation, some call it bar and bat mitzvah. When people are married, some people call it a sacrament. It was Margaret Mead, the anthropologist, who said, "When a person dies, we pretend it doesn't happen." And how important it is for you to attend the funeral, to attend the wake. You may say, "But you can't bring the person back to life." When people die, you feel the pain, the grief, but friends feel the pain, too.

People say, "But I don't know what to say." I've written twenty-one books on grief and I don't know what to say. I know what not to say. I don't say, "I know how you feel." How would I dare say this with this terrible tragedy in Oklahoma City? I don't say, "It's God's will," because no one is privy to this information. A friend of mine, Harold Kushner, wrote a book, *When Bad Things Happen to Good People.* Know what the most important word is? "When." Unanswered "whys" are part of life. When bad things happen to good people, how then do we ennoble misfortune? How do we turn an act of insanity into a gracious act for humanity? In the words of Edna St. Vincent Millay, "Grief goes on. Life goes on. I know not why." And so we go on living and sharing the path with the community of faith. And I want to tell you that one of the greatest religious experiences I have encountered is here in Oklahoma City and being a rabbi here at First Christian Church. In the midst of devastation, we are seeing people telling about God by loving each other and being in community.

This is a holy day in my faith because it is the last day of Passover. I noticed at the communion that the wafer was matzo.

It was the Last Supper of Jesus. And in synagogues throughout the world, they are reading scripture from a love story called the Song of Songs [Solomon], a love story of two people. It reads, "Behold thou art there, my love. Behold, thou art there. My beloved speaks and says to me, Rise up my loved one, my fair one and come away. For lo the winter is gone, the rain is over and past. The flowers appear on the earth and the time of singing has come, and the voice of the turtledove is heard in the land. Behold, thou art there, my love. Behold thou art there" (2:10–12, author's paraphrase). Then the writer realizes that every love story ends in tragedy. It's called death. And he concludes, "For love is stronger than the grave. Many waters cannot quench love, neither can floods drown it."

Tomorrow I return to Boston, with pain and with anguish, but also with the hope we have witnessed in a community who cared and who shared. And I will sing differently the song, "America, America, God shed his grace on thee. And crown thy good with brotherhood, from sea to shining sea." May God bless you.

Community Prayer Service

April 20, 1995
First Christian Church
Oklahoma City

Only thirty-four hours after the bombing, survivors, families of those who had been killed or who were still missing, rescue workers, and volunteers, along with hundreds of the faithful from the community at large, gathered in the sanctuary of the First Christian Church, which had become the Family Assistance Center, for an interfaith prayer service. The Oklahoma Conference of Churches sponsored the event, which included representatives from many faith traditions.

John Donne said so long ago, "No one is an island." No one stands alone. Each person's joy is joy to me and each person's grief is my own. We need one another. We come together because we cannot bear these burdens alone. We come together because in being together, we find strength and support for hearts that ache.

And we come together in prayer because we need to acknowledge that God is the source of our power and strength. We know that God's heart aches with our hearts. We know that God's heart was broken with that blast, that in fact God's will was broken with that kind of an event. And we come together to be strengthened as people of God that somehow we might minister one to another; that somehow we might be God's people to God's people.

Don Alexander, pastor
First Christian Church

Psalm 22:1–5, 9–11, 14–19, 22–24, 27–31

My God, my God, why have you forsaken
me?
Why are you so far from helping me,
from the words of my groaning?
O my God, I cry by day, but you do not
answer;
and by night, but find no rest.
Yet you are holy,
enthroned on the praises of Israel.
In you our ancestors trusted;
they trusted, and you delivered them.
To you they cried, and were saved;
in you they trusted, and were not put to
shame.

Yet it was you who took me from the womb;
you kept me safe on my mother's breast.
On you I was cast from my birth,
and since my mother bore me you have
been my God.
Do not be far from me,
for trouble is near
and there is no one to help.

I am poured out like water,
and all my bones are out of joint;
my heart is like wax;
it is melted within my breast;

my mouth is dried up like a potsherd,
and my tongue sticks to my jaws;
you lay me in the dust of death.
For dogs are all around me;
a company of evildoers encircles me.
My hands and feet have shriveled;
I can count all my bones.
They stare and gloat over me;
they divide my clothes among themselves,
and for my clothing they cast lots.
But you, O LORD, do not be far away!
O my help, come quickly to my aid!

I will tell of your name to my brothers and sisters;
in the midst of the congregation I will praise you:
You who fear the LORD, praise him!
All you offspring of Jacob, glorify him;
stand in awe of him, all you offspring of Israel!
For he did not despise or abhor
the affliction of the afflicted;
he did not hide his face from me,
but heard when I cried to him.

All the ends of the earth shall remember
and turn to the LORD;
and all the families of the nations
shall worship before him.
For dominion belongs to the LORD,
and he rules over the nations.
To him, indeed, shall all who sleep in the earth bow down;
before him shall bow all who go down to the dust,
and I shall live for him.

Posterity will serve him;
future generations will be told about the Lord,
and proclaim his deliverance to a people yet unborn,
saying that he has done it.

We pray first for those whose hearts are broken, who are suffering the death of loved ones. We pray for the injured, those who lie on beds of pain, experiencing both physical and mental anguish.

My friends, it is called upon now to offer a prayer, but in my Jewish tradition we arrive at prayer only through study. In these limited moments, I had hoped to share with you some teaching from my tradition and practice. The only text that comes to my mind—it's funny how these things work when you are in turmoil—is a movie I saw some years ago. There was a group of ten-year-old boys in a neighborhood who fear a monster in the neighborhood, a vampire or some such thing, who will destroy them. They find a strange old man who speaks with a strange foreign accent who tells them the secrets of how to defeat their evil nemesis. The boys are astonished and say, "Gee, mister, you sure know a lot about monsters." At that point, his sleeve falls down, revealing the number tattooed in the concentration camps. "Yes," he said, "I suppose I do."

I thought about that this week because I have been getting a lot of calls from Israel yesterday and today, offering me and all of us comfort. I expected them to say, "Now, you understand." What they said instead is, "Now, you don't understand." We cried together and I said, "Yes, now we don't understand, like you."

But we may learn from them a lesson that I hope will be of value. And that is that the answer to terror is courage. The answer to despair is faith. The answer to passion is wisdom. And the answer to death? We will confront and vanquish the angel of death with the weapon that is ours to use if we choose. We will confront the angel of death with life.

Rabbi Dan Shevitz
Emanuel Synagogue

Psalm 23

The LORD is my shepherd, I shall not want.
He makes me lie down in green pastures;
he leads me beside still waters;
he restores my soul.
He leads me in right paths
for his name's sake.
Even though I walk through the darkest valley,
I fear no evil;
for you are with me;
your rod and your staff—
they comfort me.

You prepare a table before me
in the presence of my enemies;
you anoint my head with oil;
my cup overflows.
Surely goodness and mercy shall follow me
all the days of my life,
and I shall dwell in the house of the LORD
my whole life long.

We pray for those who have died. They were treasured and loved and they have been cruelly taken from us. We pray for those who do not yet know and who are caught in the awful turmoil between hope and despair.

Almighty God, thou who dost hear every audible word spoken by our lips: hear also the silent moan from within us as we share the common grief and agony of having lost loved ones so unfairly . Where can we turn but to thee? We commend our loved ones into thy hands, knowing that thou art a God of love and mercy. And thus, Father, we confess that sometimes it is harder for us to commend ourselves into your hands, needing as we do now, your strength, your courage, and the power that comes only in your presence. O Heavenly Father, help us to know that only in thee can we find what we must have now. We claim it, not because we deserve it, but because, in your grace, you have offered it. In the name of our Savior, we thank you. Amen.

Dr. Gene Garrison, pastor
First Baptist Church

Isaiah 40:28–31

Have you not known? Have you not heard?
The LORD is the everlasting God,
the Creator of the ends of the earth.
He does not faint or grow weary;
his understanding is unsearchable.
He gives power to the faint,
and strengthens the powerless.
Even youths will faint and be weary,
and the young will fall exhausted;
but those who wait for the LORD shall renew
their strength,
they shall mount up with wings like
eagles,
they shall run and not be weary,
they shall walk and not faint.

Even as we meet, the search goes on. We pray for those who work and search, those who do what we cannot do because of their training, their skill, and their willingness to suffer on our behalf.

Blessed are you, Lord God. You have taught us that hope in you renews our strength. Trusting in your ever-vigilant care of us, we pray this night for the firefighters and the others who struggle to find the victims of yesterday's bombing. Strengthen their courage, Lord, sharpen their skills, steel their arms and their legs, lift them above their weariness. Move them to place their trust in you as they work in danger and in darkness. Amen.

Dr. David Wasserman, executive presbyter
Eastern Oklahoma Presbytery

Matthew 25:34–40

"Then the king will say to those at his right hand, 'Come, you that are blessed by my Father, inherit the kingdom prepared for you from the foundation of the world; for I was hungry and you gave me food, I was thirsty and you gave me something to drink, I was a stranger and you welcomed me, I was naked and you gave me clothing, I was sick and you took care of me, I was in prison and you visited me.' Then the righteous will answer him, 'Lord, when was it that we saw you hungry and gave you food, or thirsty and gave you something to drink? And when was it that we saw you a stranger and welcomed you, or naked and gave you clothing? And when was it that we saw you sick or in prison and visited you?' And the king will answer them, 'Truly I tell you, just as you did it to one of the least of these who are members of my family, you did it to me.'"

Friends, we pray for the volunteers who saw the face of need and responded immediately. And we pray for the medical personnel, whose training and skill and compassion puts them on the front lines in times of greatest need.

Almighty and eternal God, we come to you on this painful night to pray for those who continue to search through the rubble and attend the victims of this needless tragedy. Help them to bring the best of their skill, compassion, and energy. O God of tender mercies, we pray your special blessings on the doctors, the nurses and technicians, the chaplains and counselors, all those who attend to our physical and emotional and spiritual wounds. Bless their efforts, O gracious God. Let them be your hands of care and comfort. Through them work your healing, and by everything they do, may they demonstrate how much you long to restore us from our brokenness, to the end that your healing work may be done. Great and wonderful are your works, almighty and powerful God. May the efforts of these friends be among the greatest of your work this night. For we dare pray this in the name of the Lord, Jesus Christ. Amen.

Bishop Joseph Solomon
Oklahoma United Methodist Conference

Luke 13:1–5

> At that very time there were some present who told him about the Galileans whose blood Pilate had mingled with their sacrifices. He asked them, "Do you think that because these Galileans suffered in this way they were worse sinners than all other Galileans? No, I tell you; but unless you repent, you will all perish as they did. Or those eighteen who were killed when the tower of Siloam fell on them—do you think that they were worse offenders than all the others living in Jerusalem? No, I tell

> you; but unless you repent, you will all perish
> just as they did."

We pray for the perpetrators of this disaster, those whose view of live is so dark and empty that they would willingly and knowingly waste the life of another. We pray that they might come to know the awfulness of what they have done. And eternal God, we acknowledge the anguish of our hearts and souls in these moments, that we have no good answer as to why. But we do have a life-anchoring answer as to where we go from here. Into your arms we flee. Into your pathways we walk. Into the future we go, repentant for any and every act of unkindness and violence that has marked our own life and yet confident of your power to make all things new on earth and in heaven. Amen.

Bishop Robert M. Moody
Episcopal Diocese of Oklahoma

2 Corinthians 1:3–7

> Blessed be the God and Father of our Lord Jesus Christ, the Father of mercies and the God of all consolation, who consoles us in all our affliction, so that we may be able to console those who are in any affliction with the consolation with which we ourselves are consoled by God. For just as the sufferings of Christ are abundant for us, so also our consolation is abundant through Christ. If we are being afflicted, it is for your consolation and salvation; if we are being consoled, it is for your consolation, which you experience when you patiently endure the same sufferings that we are also suffering. Our hope for you is unshaken; for we know that as you share in our sufferings, so also you share in our consolation.

My friends, we pray for the survivors, those who were near the blast and yet survived. Let us pray.

Eternal God, who has always been with survivors through all the ages, be now with the survivors of this tragedy. Give them strength and courage. Give them love and hope that as their bodies begin to heal, so may their spirits find peace through you. This we ask in the name of Jesus Christ, who has given us so much, who has given us life eternal. Amen.

Ann Brackett, interim executive presbyter
Indian Nations Presbytery

1 Corinthians 13:1–2, 12–13

> If I speak in the tongues of mortals and of angels, but do not have love, I am a noisy gong or a clanging cymbal. And if I have prophetic powers, and understand all mysteries and all knowledge, and if I have all faith, so as to remove mountains, but do not have love, I am nothing....For now we see in a mirror, dimly, but then we will see face to face. Now I know only in part; then I will know fully, even as I have been fully known. And now faith, hope, and love abide, these three; and the greatest of these is love.

We come to pray for the media. They have an important job to do. May each one have balance and compassion, honoring the dignity and privacy of those who grieve.

God of Abraham and Sarah, God of Mary and Joseph, God of Priscilla and Paul: tonight we come to pray, just now, for those in local, national, and international media, as they have come to our city. Especially we pray for the reporters, the camera persons, the audio technicians, the crew members, for the long hours they give in their profession, that they give so that the whole world might know. O God, as these among us in the media share the story of our city's tragedy, may they do so with integrity, compassion, and love. In your name, O God, we pray.

Thomas R. Jewell, regional pastor
Christian Church (Disciples of Christ) in Oklahoma

Micah 6:6–8

"With what shall I come before the LORD,
and bow myself before God on high?
Shall I come before him with burnt offerings,
with calves a year old?
Will the LORD be pleased with thousands of
rams,
with ten thousands of rivers of oil?
Shall I give my firstborn for my transgression,
the fruit of my body for the sin of my
soul?"
He has told you, O mortal, what is good;
and what does the LORD require of you
but to do justice, and to love kindness,
and to walk humbly with your God?

We pray for ourselves.

O God, we are lost, we are broken. Our hearts cry out. We feel anger and frustration. We are bereft. We have been ruthlessly been cut off from those we love and cherish. Bless us, O God, that we may bless others along life's way.

O Lord, support us all this life long, until the shadows lengthen and the evening comes and the busy world is crushed, the fever of life is over and our work is done. Then in thy mercy, grant us safe lodging, holy rest, and peace at the last. Amen.

Bishop Charles Salatka, retired
Roman Catholic Archdiocese of Oklahoma City

When Senseless Violence Takes Those We Love

When senseless violence takes those we love,
and cruel death strikes childhood's promise down,
when wrenching loss becomes our bitter bread,
we know, O God, you leave us not alone.

When unexpected crises shatter life,
when those with loathing all their hate impart,
and grief becomes the fabric of our days,
dear God, you do not stand from us apart.

Our faith may flicker low and hope grow dim,
yet you, O God, are with us in our pain;
you grieve with us and for us day by day,
and with us, sharing sorrow, will remain.

Because your Son knew agony and loss,
catastrophe and grief and scorn and shame,
we know you will be with us, come what may,
your loving presence near, always the same.

Words by Joy Patterson, adapted from *Chalice Hymnal* #512 by Daniel B. Merrick and read as a poem in a candlelight vigil held in Oklahoma City several days after the bombing.
Recommended tune: SURSOM CORDA.

A Time for Healing

Oklahoma City Prayer Service, Oklahoma State Fair Arena, Sunday, April 23, 1995. Eleven thousand people crowded into the State Fair Arena for the service, while hundreds more listened from the parking lot outside. More than four thousand people gathered in the baseball stadium nearby to listen together as the service was broadcast over the loudspeakers. Thousands more gathered in nearby churches to watch the telecast together. It seemed that the only people in Oklahoma City who were not listening were the rescue teams who continued their task of searching for survivors in the rubble of the Murrah Building. Kathy Keating, Oklahoma's First Lady, organized the entire service.

Governor Frank Keating

This arena holds at most a few thousand people, but today it contains the heart of a nation. We have come here in shared sorrow to grieve the loss of beloved neighbors, to honor brave comrades, to join our souls in close communion with God.

The tragedy of April 19 shocked America. Its unspeakable evil sickened the world. Never in the history of our country have Americans witnessed such senseless barbarism. It has been suggested that those who committed this act of mass murder chose us as their victims because we were supposedly immune—the heartland of America.

Well, we are the heartland of America. Today we stand before the world, and before our God, together—our hearts and hands linked in a solidarity these criminals can never understand. We stand together in love.

We have seen the terrifying images and read the heart-touching stories. Some of us have lived them. The firefighter clutching the body of a sweet, innocent child. The policeman reaching through rubble to grasp an outstretched hand. The volunteer stretcher bearers—some black, some white, some brown, all linked in courage and compassion—rushing aid to the wounded.

The healers embracing life. The mourners lamenting death. The endless lines of donors and helpers and givers—giving their labor, their hopes, their treasure, their very blood. Through all of this—through the tears, the righteous anger, the soul-rending sorrow of immeasurable loss—we have sometimes felt alone. But we are never truly alone. We have God, and we have each other.

Today we have our neighbors—more than three million Oklahomans, and never have we drawn so close. There is something special about Oklahoma. We have always known that; now, so does America, and the world.

Today, we have our fellow Americans—from the power of our federal relief and investigative agencies to the prayers of millions. They will bring us justice as they have already brought us hope, and we will be forever grateful for this wonderful outpouring of love and support.

Today we have our families—so many of them torn by sorrow and hurt, but families still, strong through the generations, stronger yet through this terrible ordeal.

Today we have our heroes and heroines—saints in gray and blue and white and khaki—the rescuers and the healers. They have labored long and nobly. And they have cried with us.

Today we have our leaders: Mister President, Reverend

Graham, we are moved by your presence. The warmth of our welcome may be dimmed by tears, but it is one of deep gratitude. Thank you for coming to touch our lives.

Today we have our children—Oklahoma is still a young state, and our young people are very special to us. We have been brutally reminded of how precious they are by the events of the last few days. For them we reserve our warmest hugs and gentlest touch.

Today we have our God.

He is not a God of your religion or mine, but of all people, in all times. He is a God of love, but he is also a God of justice. Today God assures us once again that good is stronger than evil, that love is greater than hate, that each of us is God's special child, embraced by the Father's love.

Our pain is vast. Our loss is beyond measure. We cannot fathom this act, but we can reach beyond its horrible consequences.

The thousands of us gathered here today are multiplied by God's love, anointed by his gentle mercy. Today we are one with him, and with one another.

It is right for us to grieve. We have all been touched by an immense tragedy, and our sorrow is part of the healing process. For some of us stricken with intense personal losses, it will be a long and tortured path. For all of us it is a journey through darkness.

But darkness ends in morning light. That is God's promise, and it is our hope. There is a lovely parable of a man who looked back on his life and saw it as an endless series of footprints in the sand. At times there were two sets of footprints, side by side, and he remembered these times as happy. At others there was but one set of prints—the times of sadness and pain.

He confronted God and asked why God had ceased to walk beside him when he most needed that support. Why, he wondered, had God abandoned him?

And God answered: *But my son, those were the times I was carrying you.* He carries us today, cupped gently in his loving hands.

President Bill Clinton

Governor Keating and Mrs. Keating, Reverend Graham, to the families of those who have been lost and wounded, to the people of Oklahoma City, who have endured so much and the people of this wonderful state, to all of you who are here as our fellow Americans: I am honored to be here today to represent the American people. But I have to tell you that Hillary and I also come as parents, as husband and wife, as people who were your neighbors for some of the best years of our lives.

Today our nation joins with you in grief. We mourn with you. We share your hope against hope that some may still survive. We thank all those who have worked so heroically to save lives and to solve this crime—those here in Oklahoma and those who are all across this great land, and many who left their own lives to come here to work hand in hand with you.

We pledge to do all we can to help you heal the injured, to rebuild this city, and to bring to justice those who did this evil.

This terrible sin took the lives of our American family: innocent children, in that building only because their parents were trying to be good parents as well as good workers; citizens in the building going about their daily business; and many there who served the rest of us—who worked to help the elderly and the disabled, who worked to support our farmers and our veterans, who worked to enforce our laws and to protect us. Let us say clearly, they served us well and we are grateful.

But for so many of you they were also neighbors and friends. You saw them at church or the PTA meetings, at the civic clubs, at the ballpark. You know them in ways that all the rest of America could not.

And to all the members of the families here present who have suffered loss, though we share your grief, your pain is unimaginable, and we know that. We cannot undo it. That is God's work.

Our words seem small beside the loss you have endured. But I found a few I wanted to share today. I've received a lot of letters in these last terrible days. One stood out because it came from a young widow and a mother of three whose own husband was murdered with over two hundred other Americans when Pan Am 103 was shot down. Here is what that woman said I should say to you today:

> The anger you feel is valid, but you must not allow yourselves to be consumed by it. The hurt you feel must not be allowed to turn into hate, but instead into the search for justice. The loss you feel must not paralyze your own lives. Instead, you must try to pay tribute to your loved ones by continuing to do all the things they left undone, thus ensuring they did not die in vain. You have lost too much, but you have not lost everything. And you have certainly not lost America, for we will stand with you for as many tomorrows as it takes.

If ever we needed evidence of that, I could only recall the words of Governor and Mrs. Keating. If anybody thinks that Americans are mostly mean and selfish, they ought to come to Oklahoma. If anybody thinks Americans have lost the capacity for love and caring and courage, they ought to come to Oklahoma.

To all my fellow Americans beyond this hall, I say, one thing we owe those who have sacrificed is the duty to purge ourselves of the dark forces that gave rise to this evil. They are forces that threaten our common peace, our freedom, our way of life.

Let us teach our children that the God of comfort is also the God of righteousness. Those who trouble their own house will inherit the wind. Justice will prevail.

Let us let our own children know that we will stand against the forces of fear. When there is talk of hatred, let us stand up and talk against it. When there is talk of violence, let us stand up and talk against it. In the face of death, let us honor life. As St. Paul admonished us, let us not be overcome by evil, but overcome evil with good.

Yesterday Hillary and I had the privilege of speaking with some children of other federal employees—children like those who were lost here. And one little girl said something we will never forget. She said we should all plant a tree in memory of the children. So this morning before we got on the plane to come here, at the White House we planted a tree in honor of the children of Oklahoma.

It was a dogwood with its wonderful spring flower and its deep, enduring roots. It embodies the lesson of the Psalms—that the life of a good person is like a tree whose leaf does not wither.

My fellow Americans, a tree takes a long time to grow, and wounds take a long time to heal. But we must begin. Those who are lost now belong to God. Some day we will be with them. But until that happens, their legacy must be our lives.

Thank you all, and God bless you.

Dr. Billy Graham

President Clinton and Mrs. Clinton, Governor Keating and Mrs. Keating, Mayor Ron Norick, but most importantly of all, those of you who were in the building or injured in the bombing, or who have lost loved ones, and you from the various agencies, the fire department, medical, police, and hundreds of volunteers who are suffering because of what you have seen and felt as you have searched for the missing and cared for the injured:

No matter how hard we try, words simply cannot express the horror and the shock and the revulsion we all feel over what took place in this city last Wednesday morning. That terrible and senseless tragedy runs against the grain of every standard, every belief, every custom we hold as a civilized society, and the images of the devastation and human suffering we have seen here will be indelibly imprinted on each one of our minds and hearts as long as we live.

That blast was like a violent explosion ripping at the heart of America, and long after the rubble is cleared and the rebuilding begins, the scars of this senseless and evil outrage will remain.

But we come together here today to say to those who masterminded this cruel plot, and to those who carried it out, that the spirit of this city and this nation will not be defeated by their twisted and diabolical schemes. Someday the wounds will heal, and someday those who thought they could sow chaos and discord will be brought to justice as President Clinton has so forcefully and eloquently said. The wounds of this tragedy are deep, but the courage and faith and determination of the people of Oklahoma City are even deeper.

The Bible says in Psalm 147:3, "He heals the brokenhearted, and binds up their wounds." And so with this service today we stand together to say, let the healing begin!

But how do we understand something like this? How can things like this happen? Why does God allow this to take place?

In this section, scripture passages were quoted from memory and have been retained to keep the spirit of Dr. Graham's message.

Over three thousand years ago a man named Job struggled with the same questions. He was a good man, and yet disaster struck him suddenly and swiftly. He lost his seven sons and three daughters. He lost all his possessions. He even lost his health, his body covered with sores so unsightly that others could hardly recognize him. Even his wife and his friends turned against him.

In the midst of his suffering he asked, "Why? Why did I not perish at birth?" he cried out in his agony (Job 3:11). Perhaps that is the way you feel, and I want to assure you that God understands those feelings.

The Bible says in Isaiah 43:2, "When you pass through the waters, I will be with you....When you walk through the fire, you will not be burned; the flames will not set you ablaze."

And yet Job found there were lessons to be learned from this suffering—even if he did not fully understand it. And that is true for us as well.

What are some lessons we can learn from this tragedy? How do we understand it?

First, that it is a mystery. I have been asked on hundreds of occasions why God allows tragedy and suffering. I have to confess that I can never fully answer to satisfy even myself. I have to accept, by faith, that God is a God of love and mercy and compassion even in the midst of suffering.

I can remember many years ago lying on the dirt floor in a field hospital in Korea and looking up into the face of a soldier suspended in a frame who was horribly wounded, and asking myself, "Why?" I can recall standing at the bedside of children who were dying and asking, "Why?" I can recall walking through the devastation left by hurricanes in Florida and South Carolina and typhoons in India and earthquakes in Guatemala and California and asking myself, "Why?"

The Bible says God is not the author of evil, and it speaks of evil as a "mystery" (2 Thessalonians 2:7). There is something about evil we will never fully understand this side of eternity.

But the Bible says two other things that we sometimes are tempted to forget. It tells us that Satan is real, and that "He was a murderer from the beginning" (John 8:44). And it also tells us that evil is real, and that the human heart is capable of almost limitless evil when it is cut off from God and his moral law. The prophet Jeremiah said, "The heart is deceitful above all things and beyond cure. Who can understand it?" (Jeremiah 17:9).

That is one reason we each need God in our lives, for only he can change our hearts and give us the desire and the power to do what is right and keep us from wrong.

Times like this will do one of two things. They will either make us hard and bitter and angry at God, or they will make us tender and open, and help us reach out in trust and faith. I pray that you will not let bitterness poison your soul, but that you will turn in faith and trust to God, even if we cannot understand. It is far better to face something like this with God's strength than to face it alone and without him.

But the lesson of this event has not only been about mystery, but about a community coming together. What an example Oklahoma City and the state of Oklahoma have been to the world these past few days—and the cooperation between officials of every level no matter what religious group we belong to or what our political views may be.

None of us will ever forget the picture of a weary fireman tenderly cradling the body of a bloodstained infant, or the picture of hundreds of people standing patiently in line to donate blood. The work of the Red Cross, the Salvation Army, and a host of other humanitarian organizations, as well as the emergency workers and the doctors and nurses, have inspired us and humbled us.

A tragedy like this could have torn this city apart, but instead it has united this city and you have become a family. We have seen people coming together in a way we never could have imagined, and that is an example to us all. Hundreds if not thousands of prayer groups across the nation have arisen to pray for Oklahoma City.

The forces of hate and violence must not be allowed to gain their victory, not just in our society, but in our hearts. Nor must we respond to hate with more hate. This is a time of coming together, and we have seen that and been inspired by it.

This tragedy also gives us a lesson in comfort and compassion. We have seen an outpouring of sympathy and help not only in Oklahoma City, but from all over the nation and the world. We have been reminded that a cruel event like this, which so vividly demonstrates the depths of human evil, also brings out the best in us of human compassion and sympathy and sacrifice.

But this can also teach us about God's comfort and compassion. Some of you today are going through heartache and grief so intense that you wonder if it can ever go away. But I want to tell you that God cares, and the Bible says that he is "the God of all comfort, who comforts us in all our troubles" (2 Corinthians 1:3–4). Jesus said, "Blessed are those who mourn, for they will be comforted" (Matthew 5:4). I pray that every one of you will experience God's comfort during these days as you turn to him, for God loves you, and God shares in your suffering.

Finally—difficult as it may be for us to see right now—this event gives us a message of hope for the present, and hope for the future. Yes, there is hope. There is hope for the present because I believe the stage has already been set for restoration and renewal in this city. I am not just talking about buildings that will be repaired and rebuilt. I am talking about a new sense of community and service to each other that will endure long after the memory of this event begins to fade.

Today let all Americans rededicate ourselves to a new spirit of brotherhood and compassion, working together to solve the problems and barriers that would tear us apart.

But there also is hope for the future because of God's promises. As a Christian I have hope not just for this life but for the life to come. Someday there will be a glorious reunion with those who have died and gone to heaven before us. I believe that includes those innocent children whose lives were taken from us. I pray that you will have this hope in your heart.

This event also reminds us of the brevity and uncertainty of life. It reminds us that we never know when we too will be called into eternity. I doubt if even one of those people who walked into the Federal Building last Wednesday morning thought that it would be their last day on earth. That is why we each need to face our own spiritual need and commit ourselves to God and his will now.

It is ironic that this terrible event took place just three days after the churches in this city were filled with people celebrating Easter—just one week ago.

For the Christian, the cross tells us that God understands our suffering, for he took it upon himself in the person of Jesus Christ. From the cross God declares, "I love you, and I know the heartaches and the sorrows and the pain you feel."

But the story does not end with the cross, for Easter points us beyond the tragedy of the cross to the hope of the empty tomb. It tells us that there is hope for eternal life, for Christ has conquered death. And it also tells us that God has triumphed over evil and death and hell. This is our hope, and it can be your hope as well.

I was deeply moved Friday night when watching Larry King talking to Edye Smith, who lost her two little boys in the explosion. Her brother, a twenty-eight-year-old police officer, was dispatched to the crime scene to help, and in searching the rubble found one of his nephews. The boys' grandfather is a Christian evangelist who said that conducting their funeral is the hardest thing he has ever faced but that his faith has been crucial in helping him through the tragedy. He quoted Romans 8:28, "And we know that in all things God works for the good of those who love him" and said that if that were the only verse we had in the Bible, we could work through all our problems in life if we believed it.

President and Mrs. Clinton will remember that at the National Prayer Breakfast in Washington earlier this year, Andrew Young (who had just gone through the tragic death of his wife) closed his talk with a quote from the old hymn, "How Firm a Foundation." The fourth verse says:

> The soul that on Jesus hath leaned for
> repose,
> I will not, I will not desert to its foes.
> That soul, though all hell should endeavor
> to shake,
> I'll never, no never, no never forsake!

My prayer for you today is that you will feel the loving arms of God wrapped around you, and will know in your heart that he will never forsake you as you trust him.

Why?

Thomas R. Jewell

Rev. Jewell *is regional pastor of the Christian Church (Disciples of Christ) in Oklahoma. He made the regional office, which is next door to the First Christian Church, available to the Oklahoma Conference of Churches for planning meetings of interfaith response groups. This sermon was delivered at Southwest Christian Church in Oklahoma City, April 23, 1995.*

Psalm 121; 1 Corinthians 13

We had just finished with our devotions at the regional office of the Christian Church in Oklahoma on that Wednesday morning when a terrible noise was felt and heard throughout our building. During devotions Rev. Kathleen Logan, associate regional pastor, had been sharing a story with us, focusing on how life is like the journey up a mountain. We are constantly climbing that mountain to be in the presence of God. God throws us a rope and we make our way up, holding on to that rope. But things happen in life. We get disappointed because we didn't receive the promotion we thought we were due. We feel betrayed because a friend has let us down. Through death we lose someone who has been very close to us. On that rope that we are holding onto, these tragedies create knots, and we spend a great deal of time and energy trying to unravel them.

In these past few days we have spent a great deal of time and energy asking ourselves questions. How could anyone conceive, let alone accomplish, such a heinous crime? We ask ourselves, "Why?" Why would God permit this to happen? Unfortunately, I've heard some of the answers to these questions. I've heard one answer more often than I would care to repeat. And that is, "You know, pastor, it's God's will." In our attempt to respond to tragedy, Rabbi Harold Kushner suggests we often make the assumption that God is the cause of our suffering. And we try to understand why God would want us to suffer. Is it for our own good? Is it some sort of punishment that we deserve? Or maybe it's because God doesn't really care about God's creation. I think sometimes the answers are trying to be sensitive—they certainly are imaginative—but none are ever totally satisfying. Some lead us to blame ourselves in order to spare God's reputation, others ask us to deny reality and to repress our true feelings of anger and hate and sadness. And we are left with hating ourselves for deserving such a fate or hating God for sending it to us when we did not deserve it.

There may be another approach, however. I would like to suggest to you this morning that God does not cause our suffering. I want you to think about what David wrote in Psalm 121: "I lift up my eyes to the hills." As a young person he had been taught that sentries were somehow going to protect him or at least alert the nation of impending danger. So David in Psalm 121 says "I lift up my eyes into the hills—from where will my help come?" And then David realizes: it doesn't come from the men who stand guard. David says, "My help comes from the LORD, who made heaven and earth."

I think we want to be very clear here about the witness of David. David does not say, "My pain comes from the LORD." David does not say, "My tragedy comes from the LORD." David says, "My help comes from the LORD, who made heaven and earth."

I'll tell you, friends, we are using the phrase "the will of God" all too loosely; we're not putting it into perspective. We are dangerously bantering that phrase about when we must be specific when we use it. Much of what I say this morning comes basically from two authors, Rabbi Harold Kushner, the author of *When Bad Things Happen to Good People* and Dr. Leslie Weatherhead, who several years ago wrote a book entitled *The Will of God.*

This morning I want you to look at the cross on this communion table, and I want you to think of it in relationship to the will of God. It was not the *intentional* will of God that Christ should be crucified but rather that Christ should be followed. That's why God sent Christ to be among us. If the persons living in the time of Jesus of Nazareth had understood and received his message, repented of their sins, and realized God's kingdom—if all persons had done that, history would be very different than it is today. Those who say that the crucifixion was the will of God should remember that it was the will of evil men and women in positions of authority at that time. Period. End of story. But, when Jesus was faced with the circumstances brought about by evil and was thrust into the dilemma of whether he should run away or be crucified, then in those circumstances the cross was the will of God. It was in that sense that Jesus said it must not be what I want, but what you, my God in heaven, wants. The *ultimate* will of God in the case of the cross means that our recovery to a unity with God, a goal that would have been reached by God's intentional plan had it not been frustrated by evil, that ultimate goal will still be reached through God's *circumstantial* will. For no evil is finally able to defeat God or to cause any value to be lost.

There are two parts to the circumstantial will of God. One is very natural and one is very spiritual. God's will in the face of evil was that Jesus would be betrayed, crowned with thorns, crucified, and left to die in the blazing sun. The laws of the universe are themselves an expression of God's will and those laws were not set aside. On the cross the sword was still sharp in the side of the Savior. Christ didn't ask for the laws of nature to be repealed for him just because he was God's child. On April 19 the laws of the universe were not set aside. Pain was still pain. Falling concrete still crushed life.

But there is a spiritual side to God's circumstantial will, for Christ did not just submit to this horrible event of the crucifixion with what we might call "resignation." Dr. Weatherhead suggests that given those circumstances that evil had produced, it was God's will that Jesus should not just die like some trapped animal but that he should so react to that evil positively, creatively, as to wrest good from the evil circumstances. That is why this cross sits on our communion table. It is not the symbol of capital punishment, which it was for the Romans in the first century. It is rather the symbol of the triumphant use of evil in the cause of the holy purpose of God. If you want to talk about the will of God in Oklahoma City, look at the hundreds, thousands of people who have responded to this tragedy. There is the will of God, and don't anyone dare say that that bombing was the will of God!

Rabbi Kushner tells about a youngster who came home from Sunday school having been taught the biblical story of the crossing of the Red Sea. His mother asked him what he had learned in class. "Well, Mom, the Israelites got out of Egypt but Pharaoh chased after them. They got to the Red Sea and they couldn't cross it. The Egyptian army was getting closer and closer, so Moses got on his walkie-talkie, the Israeli Air Force bombed the Egyptians, and the Navy built a pontoon bridge so the people could cross." The mother was shocked. "Was that the way they taught you the story in Sunday school?" "Well, Mom, no, but if I told it to you the way they told it to me, you'd never believe it."

Rabbi Kushner suggests that we are like that child in the Sunday school class. We are skeptical. If anything, we find proof of God precisely in the fact that the laws of nature do not change. God has given us a wonderful, precise, orderly world, and one of the things that makes this world livable is that the laws of nature are precise and reliable and they always work the same way. Right now, because of the natural law of gravity, you are not floating about up here. But precisely because of that law of gravity, when the bomb exploded and the pillars flew away, those nine floors came crashing down. That's because the law of gravity works the same way all the time. We cannot live without gravity, but that means we also have to live with the dangers it causes. The laws of nature treat everyone alike. They do not make exceptions for good people, useful people. I am reminded of the scripture from Matthew's Gospel: "[God] sends rain on the just and on the unjust" (5:45 RSV). If you believe God gives you an umbrella, forget it! Everybody gets wet. Everybody.

There is, however, no possible situation that could ever arise which, of itself, has the power to put us down or defeat God, not even death. Today thousands of deaths are going to occur that are not what God would intend, but God will not be beaten by any possible circumstance that you could ever imagine. When a baby falls from a fifth-story window, will death be the will of God? In the sense that the laws of nature and force will function, yes. In the sense that this is what God intended, absolutely not. It was not God's will that that baby fell out of the window in the first place. Nor is disease the will of God. I think God wants perfect health for each one of us. Other things being equal, God can use a body free from disease more effectively than a diseased one. There are lots of people who are physically just fine and spiritually dead. Yet through sickness those people are awakened spiritually. In the two-angled view of this circumstantial will, there is the natural, physical condition that we call disease and tragedy and unexplainable events, and there is the spiritual side, the possibility that we can wrest from the most horrible experiences more value than could ever be known.

I don't know why one person keeps a nine-o'clock appointment and another does not. I can only assume that there are things happening that are not yet clear to me. With Rabbi Kushner I proclaim that I cannot believe that God sends illness or tragedy to a specific person for a specific reason. I don't believe in a God who has a weekly quota of malignant tumors or tragic deaths. I don't believe that God consults a divine computer to find out who is most deserving or who could handle it best. Shame on any one of us from this day forward if we should ever stand at the bed of one who is sick or sit in the living room of someone recovering from tragedy or illness and utter the words, "Well, you know, it was God's will." Shame, shame, shame on any of us so to charge the Creator of the universe.

The battle against disease, evil, and tragedy is always the will of God. Jesus certainly spoke with anger about those who would claim God's will in the ill health of anyone. Do you remember the woman who was brought to him who had been ill for a long time? Jesus spoke of her in this way, "This woman...whom Satan bound for eighteen long years" (Luke 13:16). Now as far as I can understand, Jesus, both in word and in healing miracles, taught that disease and tragedy were always part of the kingdom of evil. And with all the powers that Jesus could muster, he fought it and instructed his followers to do the same. We have witnessed, in our own community, rescue workers, health-care professionals, clergy, counselors, and volunteers doing everything possible to erase the effects of what we have experienced. And through all of this, victory is wrested from defeat and the purpose of God is realized.

I think one of the things we can say, quite frankly, is, "Well, don't you think it's a bit casual of God to allow this to happen?"

That's a reasonable question, wouldn't you say? But I have to tell you, there's a mystery here, I think we've just come to a knot in the rope. We probably have discovered the biggest knot that we will ever corporately experience in our lives. And I would not stand here this morning and say to you that I can speak of all the ways of God as if they are clear to me, because they are not. I can tell you this: I stand in the lineage of the apostle Paul, who says, "For now we see in a mirror, dimly, but then we will see face to face" (1 Corinthians 13:12).

This morning when I came out of the shower, I went over to the mirror to begin shaving. I couldn't see a thing, for the mirror was all clouded. So I took my towel and wiped the steam off. Guess what happened: it steamed right up again. Still couldn't see clearly, and I thought, "Thank you, apostle Paul," because this is what it means: we can see in the mirror only dimly, but then we shall see face to face.

We're not at the "then" time. We're not there yet. I think I will know when I'm there, and it will be a joyous day at that "then" moment. But for now, I don't despair, and I tell you why. Many came to Jesus with all kinds of questions about tragedy and evil and disease, and guess what: not all were answered. They weren't. Jesus said to Peter, "You do not know now what I am doing, but later you will understand" (John 13:7). On the night before his death he said to his apostles, "I still have many things to say to you, but you cannot bear them now" (John 16:12).

I want to tell you something this morning probably nobody has ever told you from this pulpit before. It's something that Jesus never said. Jesus never said, "I have explained the world." Jesus never said that. Not once did Jesus ever offer to explain the world. But I'm here to tell you what Jesus did say. Jesus said, "I have overcome the world" (John 16:33, RSV).

If only we could trust where we cannot see, walking in the light we have (which is very much like hanging on in the dark). If we can do faithfully that which we see to be the will of God in the circumstances that evil has thrust upon us, we can rest in the assurance that circumstances that God permits, reacted to in faith and trust, can never defeat the ultimate will of God for our lives. "For now we see in a mirror, dimly, but then we will see face to face." In the words of the contemporary poet Patrick Overton, when we walk to the edge of all the light we have and take that step into the darkness of the unknown, we must believe that one of two things will happen: there will be something solid for us to stand on, or we shall be taught how to fly! Amen.

We Have Seen the Lord

Tish Malloy

Rev. Malloy *is pastor of Village United Methodist Church. She spent a great deal of time as a chaplain volunteer at the bomb site. On Sunday, April 23, 1995, she opened the worship service by reading a pastoral letter to the congregation, excerpts of which are included here. Her sermon is from the same worship service.*

Romans 8; John 20:19–31

Many of you have gathered here to pray, and I believe that all of us have opened our hearts to God in prayer. Please know that your prayers are powerful, and continue to pray. It has been a great source of strength for me to know that your prayers are with everyone working downtown and with every family and friend affected by our shared tragedy. I have been able to say with confidence, to men and women who are often holding back tears and fighting frustration, that you are praying for them. And it does make a difference. It really helps them. I can almost see the hands and hearts of God's people holding up those brothers and sisters as they struggle to lift a brick or a body. The power of prayer is not invisible, and it is invincible.

It is important that I speak directly to you about one of the greatest gifts our God has given us in our creation, and that is the gift of *empathy.* How many of us in this past week have listened to the news or seen images that have broken our hearts out of empathy for someone else? How many of us have friends or loved ones deeply affected by the destruction that has happened in our city? I know that some of you were there in the midst of it, and you have lost dear friends and are concerned for the healing of others. Some of you are now working at the site. I know that others of you are connected by school friends who have lost parents, or work friends whose children are lost to them in this life. And still others of us empathize simply because we are connected to one another as human beings.

I must speak to you directly about this, because empathy is powerful and good. There is no shame in feeling for others. But with that statement comes a warning.

Our wellness as human beings is related not only to our bodies. Our wellness is directly linked with our spiritual and emotional well-being. To ignore or bury feelings we are having, or questions of faith we have about what has happened to ourselves or others, is self-destructive—and not in keeping with Jesus' mandate that we first love God and then love our neighbors *as* we love ourselves. And many of us do try to control our feelings by ignoring them, because we think we must be strong, and we think that strength means presenting an outward appearance that we are OK. Basic questions of faith such as "How could God let this happen?" and "How can I forgive those who have done this evil and why would God love them?" are questions that can shake us to our very core.

As your pastor, I strongly urge you to care for yourselves and others around you not only physically but also spiritually and emotionally. Our staff is now and will be prepared and ready to help you, or someone you know, through this time—and this may be for a very long time.

It's been a week that has changed us all. One thing, though, has not been shaken or moved or changed by the evil of this world, and that is the grace and love of God for everyone, the living and the dead. May we be reminded that absolutely nothing separates us from God's love and amazing grace.

Just a week ago, it was Easter Sunday. We heard the story of Jesus' friend Mary as she went to the tomb and found that the rock and rubble that sealed Christ's grave had been moved, and Jesus, her friend, was alive in a new way. After she saw him, we know that she went to tell others: "I have seen the Lord."

In the Gospel lesson we heard this morning, the disciples—even after Mary told them she'd seen Christ—hid in the upper room. Even if they did believe her, Roman soldiers were looking for Jesus' followers. Every disciple and every friend of Jesus had very good reason to be afraid for his or her life. They knew what would surely happen if they went out and began to preach as Jesus had taught them, for it did happen. All but two of the earliest disciples were eventually martyred for their faith.

And not only them, but over the ensuing two thousand years thousands of others of our brothers and sisters have lost their lives because of the evil forces of hate. In spite of their faith, in spite of God's love for them, they have suffered and sorrowed.

So in the upper room, out of love, Jesus came to his first disciples. Through the barred, locked door, Jesus came to them. In the midst of their fear and anger and confusion, Jesus came to them—and gave them and all of his disciples forever two gifts that sustain us this day.

First, he gave them peace. His greeting to them was: "Peace be with you." Second, he sent them out into the world—the world that they feared—but only after he had given them the power of his Holy Spirit. He said: I send you, in the same way that God sent me.

One of the disciples, Thomas, was absent from this experience. When he returned to his friends, they told him, like Mary had told them: "We have seen the Lord."

But Thomas had been out in the cruel and frightening world, running from shadow to shadow, hiding from people and powers that hurt and kill—cowering like a beaten dog before the harsh realities of his existence. When he heard his friends and felt the change in them—the courage in the face of fear, the faith in God's love in the midst of sorrow and loss, the hope in their spirits as opposed to the doubt in his own—Thomas simply said what made sense. He didn't decide that they were all crazy and he was the only sane disciple left. He didn't even remind them that death lay on the other side of their locked door. He simply said: I don't have that experience. I haven't seen the Lord, and I won't—I can't—believe you. I have to see him and even touch his wounds, which I know are real, for myself. Only then will I believe.

Friends, of all the disciples—of all those who so readily believed and said, "We have seen the Lord"—none can help us in these most difficult days like Thomas can.

Being a Christian in the world we live in is a challenge. It challenges our courage, our faith, and our hope. Sometimes, like Thomas, in order to believe in Christ and receive his peace, in order to feel his strength to do his work, we do need to see the Lord in a physical way—especially when our faith is tested and we are afraid or angry or confused, as many of us are right now. Especially now, we need to see the Lord and, like Thomas, we need to touch his woundedness.

That's why, while all around us we hear reports of the terrible toll that Wednesday's bomb has taken—in life and happiness and love—some of us feel compelled to help in some way, to touch the woundedness. And at the same time we also may feel helpless and unable to change a thing. Some of us, like Mary, will run to the grave and bring back good news, while others of us will go to the upper room and, in some way or other, lock the door and wait.

For some, the realization is quick. It almost seems easy for them to see God's love, in spite of the evil specter in our midst, in spite of innocence lost and grief. We hear over and over words like "If anything good could come from something like this, it is the outpouring of people's compassion and love." For some of us we can immediately say, "I have seen the Lord."

We know that in the tears of the anguished, God shares in our sorrow.

We know that in the determination of the rescuers, Christ pushes back the stones and rubble to give freedom to the bodies and souls of the lost.

We know that in the gentleness of the hands and hearts that comfort the weary and sorrowing, the Holy Spirit of God is present—and we do see the Lord.

But for others, like Thomas, our vision is clouded by the smoke of the world's hate. It's difficult to believe that God is present when evil stands before us and seems so powerful. And we are truly afraid. The truth, however, is that when we, like Thomas, run from shadow to shadow in this life, and our backs are bent and our eyes are turned away from the light—when we cannot face our fears or anger or confusion—it is difficult to see the Lord and believe. Thomas can help us with our unbelief. But more than Thomas, Jesus will.

Jesus came to Thomas, in his unbelief. He did not punish him, and he will not punish you if you are doubting today. Jesus didn't tell Thomas, "You should have believed before, and had faith." And if your faith is shaky today, he will not leave you wondering. Jesus came to Thomas and gave him what he needed. He offered to let Thomas touch his wounds and have faith, and he gave Thomas the same gifts that he gave to the other disciples. He gave them peace—and work to do, in his name. He will do the same for you and for me when and if our faith is faltering.

The good news is that God in Jesus Christ knows our human strengths and frailties, and loves us. The good news is that, through the risen Christ, we are called to live in a new way, a way of peace and a way of evil-defying action in God's world. And the good news is that by the power of God's Holy Spirit in us, we are able to move mountains of evil with love.

Go, then, and live the good news! And peace be with us all. Amen.

Resurrection in the Midst of Tragedy

C. Lawrence Bishop

Rev. Bishop *is pastor of Edmond Trinity Christian Church. Like many other clergy, he responded immediately to the crisis, offering pastoral care at Children's Hospital to parents waiting for news of their children. After receiving NOVA training, he volunteered almost full time at the Family Assistance Center as part of the death notification team. His sermon was delivered on April 23, 1995.*

Luke 24:13–35

I would say it's a pretty fair bet that most of us have been on an emotional roller coaster this past week. I actually found myself standing in the hall down at First Christian Church the other day laughing with another pastor about something and then began to feel guilty because I dared to have a moment of joy in my life.

We are absorbed in this tragedy, and yet there's something about life that keeps raising its head and saying it will take control again sooner or later. Right now, though, the pain that we're all experiencing—the fear, the uncertainty, the doubt—is pervasive. It's in our lives. We cannot and do not get away from it.

Possibly the most dramatic picture to help me illustrate is this one: Friday morning I was running late, as usual, for a workshop to help clergy understand what we will be facing over the next couple of years here in Oklahoma City. At 9:02 I was on Broadway Extension heading south near Interstate 44 when all the radio stations across the city went to a moment of silence. The newsbreaks stopped. The music stopped. There was silence.

I looked up and down Broadway Extension and virtually every car on the road had its headlights on. And I thought to myself, *this is exactly like one long funeral procession going backward and forward.* Then I realized it wasn't *like* a funeral procession at all. That's exactly what *is* happening. We are in a funeral procession right now.

There is no way to "happy talk" ourselves out of this and pretend it didn't happen. Those of us who didn't lose a friend or a relative care about someone who did. Even those of us who somehow managed to get through this without knowing anybody who was touched by the explosion have had something stolen from us that we'll never have again as long as we live: our sense of security, that it can't happen here, that Oklahoma City is somehow less of a target than New York City or Los Angeles or Washington, D.C.

We are not children anymore.

So, for a variety of reasons, we are holding a long, drawn-out funeral procession. Because we are burying so many things—not just people but our innocence as well—it's going to last a long, long time. And we are not alone.

I spoke with my mother and father in Dallas the other day. At first I thought I was reading the concern in my father's voice as concern for me. And that concern was present. But it also dawned on me as we talked that Dad was scared about Dallas. People in Portland and St. Louis and Shreveport and everywhere else around the country are probably beginning to understand it can happen wherever they live.

We're not in this alone. Somehow that doesn't make us feel any less lonely about it.

This is a time when you and I are really going to begin to have changes in our lives and in our faith. And if we are as blessed as I think and hope we're going to be, they are going to be changes of growth. I was going to use this text from Luke today, even before last Wednesday morning's events. It is a logical follow-up to Easter Sunday, how the two men walking on the road to Emmaus met Jesus, but didn't know him. We spoke of this last Sunday, how hard it is for our minds to perceive things that shouldn't be there according to what we're familiar with.

That's still a good sermon, and I'm going to preach it someday. But the situation and our needs have changed. The situation and our needs challenge the notion that a passage in the Bible means only one thing and nothing more. Friends, here is proof this is not so. What I was going to preach on is valid, and what I am going to preach on is valid. And they are not the same thing, because our lives determine the way we understand scripture. Last Wednesday morning at 8:59, I could not have seen in this scripture what I see now.

Two men were caught up in what they perceived, rightly so, as a disaster. A man was dead. One they loved was dead. It had been a citywide event. But it had a tremendous personal impact on them, for they had hoped that this man was the Messiah, the One who was going to change the world, the One they had been waiting for. And he died. Then his body had disappeared. They had heard stories, but nobody had seen him.

Then Jesus approached them, but because of their inability to see what they didn't expect to see, they missed him. They did not know who he was. They had been expecting the Messiah to come in a different way—certainly not as a crucified man. Certainly they weren't prepared for this kind of resurrection.

And so they walked with him and they talked and Jesus taught them. He explained to them what the prophets had meant. He was a rabbi first and foremost and he taught them. Still, they didn't recognize him. Having a rational explanation of seemingly irrational events does not always help us understand what is going on.

Jesus walked with them and taught them. He was very visible and very personal. And for all of that, they still didn't know him.

But then there came a moment, a familiar moment, in which he took a loaf of bread and broke it. Now, we don't know if they were there at table with him on the night when the Lord's Supper was instituted, the night when he was betrayed. We don't know; maybe they were, maybe they weren't. Breaking of bread was a very traditional thing; you did it every day. And then he offered them wine.

They ate and they drank a regular meal. It's important for us to understand that at this moment they were not serving him, but he was serving them. At that moment, he offered them sustenance, he offered them care. He offered them love. He ministered to them.

At that moment they perceived him.

File that away for a moment. We'll bring it back in before we're done.

We need to talk, you and I. We can't do it all today. This experience is going to be with us for the rest of our lives. Every one of us will relive this and we will carry it with us. It will weigh less as time goes on but it is a part of who we are from this day forward. Like it or not, what we've got to learn is, not to like it, but at least to accept it. And we need to talk about how we do this. We need to talk about theology too. And there are some things I need to share with you about that, this first Sunday.

I have heard people say this week, and you probably have too, that somehow this is God's plan. For some reason this had to happen so something else, something good, could happen.

That, my friends, is blasphemy! This was not God's plan. Not my God and I hope not yours. Now you may say, "God is God! There is only one God!" But who we perceive God to be really informs how we approach God, how we understand God, whom we worship.

And to say this is not God's plan does not say for a minute that God does not *have* a plan. But *this* isn't it. Too often in human experience, you and I take a look at something where God has managed to create something good out of tragedy and we see that even out of the ashes something wonderful has happened. And we say, "Oh! God let that happen so this could happen."

No! No! No! No! No!

God is a creative God. God does not destroy. God may come across the destruction and enter into it with us, but God is always building, always creating. The ability to make a silk purse out of a sow's ear does not imply the seamstress created the sow's ear.

There is an evil, destructive force in this world. We Disciples don't talk about it too much. But it is there. I don't know what it is. I don't know how to describe it. I don't know for sure what to call it. But we have seen it time and again in human history. And we met it personally last Wednesday morning. Whatever it is touched the hearts of a few young men, and maybe women, and maybe not all of them so young. Whatever that is, it brought about the destruction.

Our God is a creative God who will build from this. But don't let anyone tell you that God created this. God doesn't work that way!

We need to talk, you and I, about what's going to happen three months from now, and six months from now, and the different ways this stress is going to play itself out in our lives and in the lives of our families and in the lives of our friends. And we'll talk about it some through sermons, we'll talk about it some through classes, through workshops, through handouts, through newsletter articles. I don't know. We'll have to figure that out as we go, because none of us have been down this road before.

But today we need to understand one thing first and foremost. There will be a time of healing for you and me. But right now is a time to hurt. There's going to be a time where we're going to pick up our lives and get on. Right now we need to grieve, we need to be in that funeral procession. It's OK! Because even as we are starting to put our lives back together, we know that the work is just beginning.

There's going to be a time for forgiveness, not just for the benefit of the evildoers, but for our own sakes, so that our lives do not become embroiled in hate and rage and anger, so that we don't lose focus of the good things of life, so that we don't lose hope and kindness and faith.

But right now, it's OK to be angry. Evil has invaded our world, and we are allowed righteous anger.

There will be time for these things to come, but feel where you are now. Know this is something that isn't easily forgiven. Know this is something we will not easily recover from. Accept it. Live with it. Because if you fool yourself, you will lose hope.

Somehow, we've got to embrace this thing and accept it. We don't want to. But we have to.

William Sloane Coffin tells a story. I want to share part of it with you, because it is a story about our God. His very real and very personal story tells of the death of his son on a cold night, driving into a body of water. Afterward, some people wondered how God could let that happen. Some said that God was calling him home. Others said it was God's plan. But Coffin knew what you and I really know—that when that car hit the water, God's heart was the first to break.

Last Wednesday morning at 9:02, God's was the first heart to break.

That's the understanding we need to begin with. The fact that God is here. That God has done nothing to harm us, or anyone we love. That God has not deserted us.

God's heart is breaking with ours. God wants us whole and healthy. God wants to minister us back to health. Certainly God wants us to be loving, forgiving Christians, but God knows we are human beings, too.

Let's begin with that, you and I, as we face these next several weeks, understanding that God is here, God loves us, God is going to heal us. And know that God has accepted the children and the others who have died into something that is far greater than anything you and I have ever known. Let's start there!

We know this is true, because two thousand years ago, two men were walking along a dusty road, feeling some of the tragedy and despair you and I are feeling now. And God came to them in the form of the resurrected Christ, and walked with them. They didn't see Christ with them. But through Christ's ministry they saw him with them. And they knew God loved them.

God is with us also! And God loves you.

Thanks be to God! Amen.

The Greatest Power of All

John A. Petusky

Fr. Petusky is a pastor of the Catholic Parish of St. John the Baptist in Edmond. He is immediate past president of the Oklahoma Conference of Churches. He was the leader in both planning and participating in crisis response and grief management training for local clergy. His sermon to the children was preached on the occasion of their first communion,
April 23, 1995.

Children, I'd like for you to think of the most powerful thing in the world. There is, of course, electricity, which we think can do almost anything. There is nuclear fission, which you will learn about in science class, which is at the very heart of all of creation, and very powerful. There is the sun in the sky, which seems to make everything grow. There is water, which can be very powerful. Then there are the forces of nature, like a hurricane, a thunderstorm, or an earthquake. They are very powerful, as well. There is even evil. We have experienced some of that this week, have we not?

Evil can be very powerful and it can touch us. Just a few weeks ago, I was talking to the confirmation class and I warned them about evil people—people like drug dealers who kill souls, people like the wicked ones who killed and hurt so many people in our community this week, people who hate and who do violence.

But today, I want to tell you about a power that is greater than all of these—greater than nature, greater than electricity, greater than nuclear fission, and yes, a power that is even greater than evil. And that is the power of God's love. Because, you see, all of creation is created by this God. It came from God's hand.

There is a beautiful picture in the Vatican. It is painted on the ceiling. It shows God's hand reaching out. And it shows Adam reaching toward that hand. The two hands almost touch. And God is giving his life; God is giving his power to our ancient ancestors, Adam and Eve, our first mother and father.

Now, God wants you to have this power, this love of his. And he wants you to know about it. So what did God do? He sent his beloved Son. The scriptures put it very beautifully. "God so loved the world that he sent his beloved Son, that all who believe in him will have eternal life." The Father sent Jesus to send us a message of his love and his power that is greater than any earthly force and that is even greater than evil.

Jesus came and he spoke to us often of God's love. He came and told us how we aren't God's servants or God's slaves. No, he told us that we are God's friends, the children of God. And perhaps many years ago, or perhaps just a few, God gave us all his life in baptism. Jesus put that powerful life in the eternal life that will never end. You see, God's power will overcome all other powers, even evil. And all that can remain must be God's love.

Jesus did something very important. He wanted us to have that love; he wanted that love to be within us. So he gave us the Holy Eucharist. Let me ask you children, and you can all answer with one voice, because I think you know the answers. Is the bread that we will receive just plain bread? [No.] It is what?

[The body of Jesus Christ.] And the cup of wine, is it just some wine? [No.] It is the what? [The blood of Christ.]

By the power of his Spirit Jesus puts his very life, his very power, within the Holy Eucharist. It is no longer merely bread and wine. It has more power in it than nuclear fission has, because it is the love of God and the love of God can overcome anything.

I was just thinking this week about the terrible event and how much good God brings even from that evil. Think of the many kind and generous and loving people who are showing compassion and care. Also think, and always remember this in your life, that on the other side of that destruction was God saving these people and giving them his life. For he has died to save all people and they are safe in the Father's hands. And that is why we celebrate today with sad hearts for friends and family members who have perhaps gone. But it is important to remember that God has saved them and they are safe and well in his hands.

We must never in life doubt God's love because it is the most powerful thing. It can overcome hate. It can overcome any evil. God wants us to trust him, to believe in him. And that love and that power, my dear children, is coming to you today. You will receive that power in your hands and take it with your lips. And Jesus will come and live in you and will give you that power so that you can believe in him, so that you can trust in him and so that you can love him. You should never be afraid. Whatever happens in your life, all you have to do is turn to the God of love and he will love you and give you his mercy and give you his life.

If I would ask you to describe in some way how much God loves us, the cross is the very best symbol of that. How much does God love us? This much. God gave us his Son, who gave everything for us, and then put his life in the bread and the cup that we might have that life as well.

May I just take a moment to talk to the adults?

We have a tremendous treasure in these children of ours. We all know this week when we sensed the horror of the children how aghast we were. We were angry that any kind of violence would happen, but we could not believe that anyone would harm the little ones, those most precious gifts of God. And how much we must realize what a treasure human life is. For it is the vessel of eternal life. It is where God puts his eternal life. And how much we must cherish the life God gives to us and how we must care for it.

I would like all the children taking their first communion to come up on the altar steps now. Turn and face your families. We want these children to know how precious they are to us. So we are going to pray over them today. Parents, grandparents, brothers and sisters, let us hold our hands out over them.

O Lord our God, send your powerful love upon these children. Protect them from harm. Today they will become vessels of the Eucharist. You will live in their hearts, in their minds, in their bodies. Give them faith. Give them strength. Give them most of all, Lord, families who love them, adults who witness to them. Bless them, Lord. Protect them. Give them your love. We ask this through Christ, our Lord. Amen.

Reflections on a Nightmare

Bill Simms

Rev. William Simms *is pastor of the Wildewood Christian Church, a unique congregation in two locations, Wildewood and Wildewood/ University Place. He received NOVA (National Organization of Victim Assistance) training and was a chaplain volunteer. This sermon was delivered on April 23, 1995.*

Mark 5:1–14

I'm not really going to preach today. I just want to make a few observations about my reflections on the tragedy that occurred at the Federal Building. These comments may not be logical or sensible, but neither was this event logical or sensible.

In talking with people, I've heard many different kinds of comments. I've heard individuals express different types of feelings—such as anger, helplessness, confusion. It's all right to be angry. I mean, it's natural, when something like this happens, that you feel anger. It's instinctive to feel that way, but don't maintain your anger, don't carry that anger with you from now on, because it will destroy you if you do.

I've had some people who have talked to me about the way that they felt. They said, "Am I crazy, feeling the way I feel?" I said, "No, you are not crazy. The people who did this—they are the crazy ones."

You know, it's very sane for us to respond in the way that we have responded because something out of the ordinary has happened. Something we can't explain has happened. Something that defies all laws of logic and common decency has happened. Something that we don't see every day has happened. The rug has been snatched out from under our feet because we've always prided ourselves on the fact that we were safe and secure here in America.

A lot of folks have asked, "How in the world could this happen? How in the world could someone do this?" I think that our scripture for today, Mark 5:1–14, gives us a lot of answers to that question. You see, we live in a world where the demonic is very much present. I know that some folks have denied the existence of Satan, but after seeing what's happened here, I don't know how anybody can say there is no devil. Nothing but a demonic, satanic force could do what was done on April 19.

When somebody gets the devil in him, he will do anything. When the devil is in you, you are no longer functioning on your own. The devil is functioning through you. You know how they arrest people sometimes. When you are driving under the influence, they say that you no longer have control. You no longer have control of those things you normally have control over, such as your reflexes. The person who did this was operating under the influence of Satan. This thing was demonic, there is no way around it. When you find people who are filled with the devil, they will do anything. They just don't care. They have no principles; they don't care whom they hurt.

I want to make sure though that we realize how the devil operates because I even heard some folks say, "Well, it was the

Lord's will." No! No! No! This was not the Lord's will. This was the will of some evil, sinful, demonic people. This was their will. It's not the Lord's will. The Bible tell us that Satan, the devil, comes like a thief to steal, to kill, and to destroy. Jesus said, "I came that [you] might have life, and have it abundantly" (John 10:10). Don't tell me that the God I serve, the God who created this world, is interested in destroying the lives of innocent people and killing babies. No! Not the God I serve. Jesus said, "Let the little children to come to me, and do not stop them; for it is to such as these that the kingdom of heaven belongs." Again Jesus said, "If any of you put a stumbling block before one of these little ones who believe in me, it would be better for you if a great millstone were fastened around your neck and you were drowned in the depth of the sea." So don't tell me this was God's will. This is not what God wanted. This was the will of somebody operating under the influence. The devil is good at throwing rocks and hiding his hands. He is good at having us blame God for what he has done. He wants you to blame God, he wants you to question God, and he wants you to make God responsible for what has happened.

I know that you feel down and out, sad, angry, disappointed, and discouraged. Those are the emotions that the devil likes to see. We know that some of that is going to be natural for a while, just don't stay there with it. You see, in spite of this isolated incident—and that's what it is, an isolated incident—God's folks are still going to win. The devil wants you to think you've been defeated. He wants you to think that because a few folks did this the whole world is evil, and that's not true. This is an isolated incident and we are still going to claim God's victory.

You know some folks are saying that this occurred because people are upset about what happened in Waco, Texas, two years ago. This was their sad and evil way of commemorating the second anniversary of that event. I tell you there was more to it than that. I tell you Satan wants to steal our joy. What was last Sunday? Last Sunday was a Sunday of victory. Last Sunday was Easter Sunday. Satan somehow wants to come and steal our joy; he is trying to take away our victory, and he is trying to make us forget about what we celebrated last week. We need to tell him that he is not going to do it. In spite of what happened, we are still going to trust God.

No matter what you do, Satan, we still know you are nothing but a liar, a thief, and a murderer. We will not let you take away our joy. We are going to survive with a joyful spirit in spite of what happened. You see, Satan, we know something that you evidently are not thinking about: even though you may take somebody's life, the God I serve can either keep us from death or he keeps us in death. The God I serve will walk with us, even though we walk through the valley and the shadow of death. We don't have to fear any evil, because God is with us.

We know that it is possible for a man to sneak beyond the guard of the Secret Service and take the life of President John Kennedy. We know that is possible for a man with a pistol to sneak beyond the guard of the Secret Service and kill Robert Kennedy. We know that a man can take the life of Martin Luther King, Jr., while he was on a motel balcony. We know that a man with a truck bomb can take the lives of many folks in Oklahoma City. But no one can sneak beyond the protective arm of God and take the soul of one of God's children.

Let me tell you something: one day those destroyed in the bombing will rise again and then we are going to have the victory. Satan wants you to think that you have lost, but you have won. He can do some things and some things he can't. Even though I have to live in a Good Friday world, I know that my real joy is Easter. That's my real day, Easter. I may live in a Good Friday world where evil men and women are all around, and where evil folks do evil things, but I know that our real joy is Easter. The devil can't destroy that.

One thing this event has helped us do is to get some things into focus. Some of the things we thought were so important don't seem so important anymore. Some of the things we've been banking on don't mean so much right now. I haven't seen too many people since this happened go down to the bank and count out their money to see how much they have. I haven't seen folks comparing their cars, deciding whether they want bigger and better cars. Those things don't mean so much right now. This tragedy has helped us get a better perspective on life. Things we once took for granted aren't as secure as we thought they were.

There are so many reflections being made about this event. However, we shouldn't always try to come up with the easy answer. One easy answer is to say, "Well, it was God's will." But it was not God's real will. It could have been his circumstantial will, as a result of what we've done, but it was not God's will.

We come up with so many simple answers, and some of the answers are even silly. I heard a very high official say, "We are going to see that this never happens again." Well, that's stupid. I mean, how can you see that this doesn't happen again? There is no way in the world that somebody can watch everybody. There's no way in the world you can stop some nut from doing some nutty thing, especially if he is operating under the influence of Satan. There's no way that anyone can see that it never happens again.

Now what we can do is try to create a world, an environment, a community, a church, and a neighborhood where these things are less likely to happen. The only way this can be accomplished is by the transformation of lives. We must take children while they are young, and before they get hate in their minds, and deal with them and work with them. Only then can you create a spiritual environment—one that gives people a conscience, gives people a sense of right from wrong. Then you can lessen the chances of this type of tragedy happening again.

Some have said that this is God's wake-up call. God may use this to help wake us up, but I won't say this is God's wake-up call. To say that this was God's way of waking us up, No! No! God may use what has happened to make us better people, to make this a better world, but God didn't cause the bombing. This was not his idea of a wake-up call.

All of those people who went to the Federal Building on April 19—who went to work, or who went to the Social Security office, or who were dropped off at the day-care center—went there not knowing that they would not return. You know what that says to me? That life is uncertain. It says that you never know what a day is going to bring. Not only do you not know what a day is going to bring, you don't even know what the next hour is going to bring.

Folks, since we don't know what a day is going to bring, since we don't know what the next hour is going to bring, we ought to live each moment as if it were our last. Don't you know that life is too short to be mad at somebody? Life is too short to go through it with a chip on your shoulder. Life is too short to go through it dwelling on the mundane things. Life is too short to go through it majoring in minors. Life is so short that we need to get busy building God's kingdom, saving souls, transforming lives, and picking people up out of the gutter. We've got to get busy for the Lord. When you leave home, you need to leave home right. When you leave home you may be angry with your children, but you still need to go and hug them before you leave. You never know if you're going to have that chance again.

I remember in the sixties, when we were participating in the civil rights marches, there was a song we would sing as we would march. We would sing to lift spirits because sometimes police dogs were there, fire hydrants were there, sometimes there were angry mobs out there wanting to attack us, and sometimes even the policemen wanted to beat us. We used to sing that old song

"This may be the last time, children, I don't know, it may the last time we shout for joy; it may be the last time, children, I don't know; it may be the last time we walk for Jesus, it may be the last time."

If you think about those words and the tragedy of April 19, we should be mindful that this may be the last time, church, we don't know—this may be the last time we come together, we don't know. This may be the last time we pray together, we don't know. This may be the last time we fellowship together, we don't know. This may be the last time we hug one another, we don't know. This may be the last time we shake hands with each other, we don't know. Since I don't know, I want to make sure that everything is all right. For if this old body of mine is destroyed, and goes back to the dust from whence it came, I want to make sure that even without this body, as Job said, I shall see my Redeemer, I shall see my God, face to face. This may be the last time, we don't know.

Another song we used to sing through the marches was "I want Jesus to walk with me, all along this tedious journey, I want Jesus to walk with me." That's the thing I can say to anybody. I don't care if you lost a loved one, I can still say: Jesus will walk with you. I don't care what has happened, if somebody in your family was wounded, I can tell you that God is present with you. I can tell you that God wants to help and I can tell you that before your heart broke, God's heart also broke. I can tell you before you experienced your pain, God was also experiencing that pain. God is with us in the midst of this tragedy. God is with us in the midst of all that has happened. We ought to say, "I want Jesus to walk with me."

Another verse in that same song says, "When I am sick, I want Jesus to walk with me." And a verse says, "When I'm dying, I want Jesus to walk with me." I don't know about you, I don't know how long you'll be here, and I don't know how long I'll be here. All I know is my time on this earth is not as long as it was when I came into the world. Even when I am dying, when everything is gone, and I don't have anything else, I want Jesus to walk with me. Walk with me, Lord. Walk with Oklahoma City. Walk with all of us.

Dwelling in the Safety of His Wings

Jim Hylton

Rev. Hylton *is senior pastor of Metro Church, a nondenominational fellowship in Edmond. He had just begun his ministry when the disaster struck. His challenge was to minister to the congregation when he had not yet moved into his home.*

Psalm 91:1–16

Last Wednesday morning at approximately 9:00 a.m. a terrorist bomb exploded in front of the federal building in downtown Oklahoma City. The enormous explosive power of the bomb sent one third of the building crashing downward. Shock waves that followed have reached all of us. It is the most violent act of terrorism in our nation's history.

This event seems like a horror movie that will surely end soon so we can wind our way out of the theater to a world of reality free from the heaviness that presses on our hearts. Amid the flying debris are the many questions that arise. God's word answers these questions for people who see things with eyes of faith.

Who would do such a dastardly deed? Only the devil can conceive such a scheme and create such a weapon of indiscriminate violence. Jesus set the record straight: The devil came as a thief to kill, steal, and destroy. He said in bold contrast: I have come to give you life and give it more abundantly (John 10:10, paraphrase). The Bible speaks of the mystery of iniquity. That mystery is the insidious and diabolical nature of evil and sin that is spawned in the human heart. Behind the deeds of this atrocity is the desire of the devil to kill and destroy, then leave people in the prison of fear and dread.

How could God allow this to happen? God has never violated human free will. He has allowed the operation of the enemy until he casts him from the earth in the end time. God's provision is to guide us to know his protection. This protection was completed in Christ's life, death, and resurrection.

Some would raise the question of fairness. Is it fair for God to allow the devil access to people's minds to plot and execute such a deed? We do not have will without a choice. That choice was present on the earth since the devil plotted the downfall of woman and man in the garden. Two trees were named in the garden, the tree of life and the tree of knowledge of good and evil, giving the first humans a choice.

It was not fair for Jesus to die, yet God allowed his son to die for our sins that we might have eternal life. Fairness is not the issue. The issue is redemption. God redeems us out of our circumstances and tragedies.

Many people were protected and survived, just as we have heard in the testimony of Wayne this morning. While some escaped physically, all who are in Christ escaped into heaven. The provision of Christ for both the dead and the living is a complete provision. Those who die in the Lord do not regret their quick departure to be with him. Those who live will have the greater challenge.

A friend of mine who distinguished himself as a lawyer and

then a banker tells of surviving almost certain death in World War II. A "suicide plane" struck his ship, killing many of his crew. He was expected to die also, and had an out-of-body experience. In that time he was aware of the Lord and saw heaven in the distance. Many times he has related to me the sense of destiny and purpose that is behind his life as a survivor. He is not his own, just as none of us are. We all owe our lives to another. We have all been bought with a price.

How do we help the survivors and the victims' families? Already the outpouring of compassion and love has surrounded people. While villains will forever etch their names in infamy, heroes have emerged who will remain "what's her name?" Line up those who engaged in the insane thinking leading to these deeds of darkness and they will be few. Line up the heroes who dropped what they were doing to go to the scene and begin the rescue efforts and they will stretch out across the state.

Our church family was part of leading the way. The staff took strategic positions at the site and in the hospitals. Our members that are part of the medical community have given their skills and their knowledge of God's power and ability to heal. Countless volunteers have taken food, clothing, and other needed services to people. Emergency funds are being given and collected here. Funds are coming from Clark Whitten's new place of ministry, Calvary Assembly of God, Orlando, and from other churches outside the state.

John Perkins said, "The church is at her best when as the community of faith, she wraps her arms around the community of pain." The arms of this community of faith have been and will continue to be stretched out about the community of pain.

Our rights to the throne of God in prayer must be exercised. "God hath not given us a spirit of fear; but of power, and of love, and of a sound mind" (2 Timothy 1:7 KJV). We can pray for people to be freed of fear. We are to pray for God to give us his power. His power visiting the victims and their families will strengthen them from within. His power visiting our city will bring us all together.

We are to pray for his love. His love is poured out in the Holy Spirit. As we pray for the love of God to saturate lives and to bring a canopy over the city, we can expect fear to flee. Perfect love casts out fear. We are to pray for sound thinking. Many thoughts vie for people's attention in these times. Wisdom is to be claimed from God. Wisdom is needed for those who have lost loved ones. Wisdom is needed for those still engaged in the rescue and the care of the injured. God's wisdom is needed in the city, and the nation as well, as we address how to prevent such a tragedy from occurring again.

Will our lives be lived in a sense of dread? God has provided us a security system! The psalmist knew well the security of abiding in the shadow of the Almighty. Our refuge is the Lord himself. Christ is in us as Christians. We are in Christ as Christians.

Every Christian was attended by the Lord's presence in the bombing. Even now the presence of the Holy Spirit is with the bodies of Christians who have not been removed from the debris. The biblical account of that reality is the record of the body of Elisha in the grave. A grave was hurriedly dug at the end of a battle and the body of a casualty was placed in the grave of Elisha. The Holy Spirit operating in power in Elisha's life was still present with the body in death and the soldier being buried was resurrected (2 Kings 13:20–21).

We are to accept his provision. The psalmist personalized this privilege, saying, "He is my refuge and my fortress, my God, in whom I trust" (NIV). It is necessary for us to choose God's provision in Christ. We must enter in through trusting Jesus personally. Everyone can declare as the psalmist does, "He is my refuge and my fortress."

We can claim his covering. An unusual analogy is presented. It is the picture of a mother bird enfolding her young under her wings. The psalmist said, "He will cover you with his feathers, and under his wings you will find refuge" (NIV). His covering wings connote warmth and love in the soft down of his goodness and grace.

Jesus looked at Jerusalem and prayed, saying, "Jerusalem, Jerusalem,...how often I have longed to gather your children together, as a hen gathers her chicks...but you were not willing" (NIV). I can hear him saying today, "Oklahoma City, Oklahoma City, I am seeking to gather you under my wings as a mother hen gathers her chicks." I believe that out of this event our city will be gathered under the wings of Christ.

We can face the future with hope and confidence. Times like these press us into Christ with greater assurance. The inscription on a church in England reads: "In the year 1653, when all things sacred in the kingdom were either profaned or demolished, this church was built to do the best of things in the worst of times." Our church is rallying to do the best of things in the worst of times, as is the entire community of life-giving churches throughout Oklahoma City.

The psalmist knew this confidence: "If you make the Most High your dwelling—even the LORD, who is my refuge—then no harm will befall you, no disaster will come near your tent. He will command his angels concerning you...so that you will not strike your foot against a stone" (NIV).

Our nation has become a nation filled with weapons because of the rampant escalation of violence. We must not and will not be taken hostage to unforgiveness and hatred. Our weapon is to love and give our lives in service in the name of Jesus.

Joseph Song is credited with the overthrow of the evil government of Romania. His church grew and grew until his life was threatened. When threatened with a gun and his own death he said, "Your weapon is killing, my weapon is dying. If you use yours, I will be forced to use mine." Those threatening him knew that their weapon could take his life, but his weapon would rally and inspire a nation. "The weapons of our warfare are not carnal, but mighty through God to the pulling down of strongholds; casting down...every high thing..., and bringing...every thought to the obedience of Christ" (2 Corinthians 10:4–5 KJV). Paul's understanding of God's protection caused him to conclude that to live was good, but to die was gain!

We gather here on a day of remembering the victims and their families, to draw near to God knowing he will draw near to us. We can know his soft, downy wings are about us, causing our hearts to know comfort and hope.

When John Owen, the great Puritan, lay on his deathbed, his secretary wrote (in his name) to a friend, "I am still in the land of the living." "Stop," said Owen. "Change that and say, 'I am yet in the land of the dying, but I hope soon to be in the land of the living.'" We are still in the land of the dying. Many have gone on to the land of the living. Someday we will join them. For us now there is his comfort, his hope, and his strength to meet our needs and to enable us to serve others.

Triumph in the Midst of Trouble

Dr. M. L. Jemison

Rev. Jemison *is pastor of St. John Missionary Baptist Church. He is chairman of the Oklahoma City Christian Relief Fund and serves nationally as Second Vice President of the two-and-a-half million member Progressive National Baptist Convention. He served as a volunteer chaplain at the bomb site. His sermon was preached to his congregation on April 23, 1995.*

Psalm 46

This week has tested many of us. In fact, it has tested all of us to the depths and limits of our faith and our ability to perceive and understand. We all looked with pain and passion at the horrific dismantling of a structure that served as a workplace, as well as a reference place, for family, friends, neighbors, colleagues, coworkers, schoolmates, social workers, and church members.

A surge of emotion floods us, ravaging our psyche and sanity as we look somberly at the most gross display, to date, of a person's inhumanity to other people. Well, although this week—a week of tragedy, horror, pain, disbelief, agony, discouragement, disdain, hope, and despair—has been a bitter pill to swallow, the Lord says, the Bible teaches, and yesterday's experiences affirm our testimony and reveal that we can triumph in the midst of trouble.

The secret we all need to discover is how to react to troubles, what we can learn from them, and how God helps us in the midst of them. Jesus did not promise a life devoid of trouble, but an untroubled heart. "Let not your hearts be troubled," he challenged (John 14:1). An untroubled heart can triumph over troubles based on three firm convictions: The Lord is on our side, by our side, and gives us peace inside.

Hezekiah was king over Judah. The Northern Kingdom had already fallen to Sennacherib, the Assyrian conqueror. Now he was on his way to Egypt, conquering and capturing cities and territories in his path. The little kingdom of Judah stood in his way. In the year 701 B.C., the fearsome general ravaged the small city of Lachish. Then he sent a message to Hezekiah saying, "That's exactly what I'm going to do to Jerusalem."

Talk about trouble! Hezekiah had his. But what he did with Sennacherib's troublesome warning gives us the first key as to what to do when trouble hits us. Hezekiah took the letter and spread it out before the Lord in the temple. Isaiah came to him and warned him not to enter into any alliance to save Jerusalem but to trust in the Lord only.

The Assyrians advanced to Jerusalem as Sennacherib had warned. They camped around the city walls and prepared to attack the city. The battle was set to begin at midnight. Everyone in Jerusalem waited, gripped by fear.

Then it happened. A mysterious plague swept over the Assyrians and one hundred eighty thousand of them died. At five minutes before twelve, those who were still alive retreated. Sennacherib returned to Nineveh beaten, not by combat with Judah's armies or the strong walls of Jerusalem, but by the Lord's intervention. The holy city was saved.

Well, the God who rescued Hezekiah from this grim and terrifying situation can also enable us, empower us, and enlighten us as we struggle to gain some semblance of understanding about this week of trial and tribulation.

I have heard those touched by this situation say, over and over again, how overwhelming it is, how inadequate they feel, how violated they feel, how angry they feel. You're all right! I dare not come to you with a cut and dried philosophy about this senseless tragedy. I dare not come to you suggesting that you suppress your emotion, bury your pain, or ignore your feelings. But I do stand before you this morning proclaiming God is able. God will make a way. God is our refuge and strength.

You see, trouble time is turning time. The psalmist says, "I will lift up my eyes." Trouble time is trusting time. Solomon says, "Trust in the Lord with all your heart." Grandma sang, "I will trust in the Lord until I die." Trouble time is the right time for us to affirm our faith and stay in the race. Here Psalm 46 teaches three things about God.

1) *God is on our side.* That is the meaning of these familiar, oft-repeated words:

> God is our refuge and strength,
> a very present help in trouble (verse 1).

The Hebrew means a "high tower or protection place." The Lord is one to whom we can retreat for refuge and from whom we receive strength in trouble. Just as Hezekiah spread out before the Lord the threats of Sennacherib, so too, the first thing to do when trouble strikes is to pray.

Prayer enables us to see the issues of our trouble and seek the Lord's guidance. There is a silver lining in every situation when you look at it from God's point of view. All trouble has some troubled person causing it. Often the Lord uses the trouble to get to us so that through us he can get to the people involved.

When we pray, he gives us the vision of how we are to act and what we are to say. He prepares the way before us, opening doors of opportunity. He helps us to know his timing. To fully understand the tragedy of this week, we will have to back away from it and make our way to God. Retreating from the trouble into communion with him provides the wisdom, insight, and courage we need to know what to do and when to do it. Like Hezekiah, there is little we can do except trust that the Lord will intervene to help us when we face impossible, insurmountable odds.

The psalmist's description of the Lord as a "present help in trouble" in Hebrew means, "One willing to be found." Isaiah 55:6 expresses it this way: "Seek the LORD while he may be found, call upon him while he is near." To seek the Lord is the direct result of the fact that he has found us and calls us to belong to him so that we can be free to call upon him.

2) *God is by our side.* The psalmist is declaring that God is both a retreat from trouble and a strength in the midst of it.

> Therefore we will not fear, though the earth
> should change,
> though the mountains shake in the heart
> of the sea;
> though its waters roar and foam,
> though the mountains tremble with its
> tumult (verses 2–3).

The psalmist speaks here of a shaking situation. Right now, we are in the midst of a shaking situation. We are uncertain about life and uncertain about death. All we know is that somebody is missing about us, and around us there is crumbling.

The psalmist says if the foundation be destroyed, what then? We can't live without fear until we know that nothing—not what people do or say, not the disappointing reversals of life, physical sickness or pain, not even death—can ultimately hurt us or destroy our relationship with the Lord and his promise that we will live with him forever. Fearlessness comes not only from knowing God is on our side, but also that he is by our side.

> There is a river whose streams make glad the
> city of God,
> the holy habitation of the Most High.
> God is in the midst of the city; it shall not be
> moved;
> God will help it, when the morning
> dawns.
> The nations are in an uproar, the kingdoms
> totter;
> he utters his voice, the earth melts.
> The LORD of hosts is with us;
> the God of Jacob is our refuge (verses 4–7).

These words are rich with imagery. The river is symbolic of the presence of God. The Holy Spirit of the Lord is with us to sustain us. We are never alone. Hezekiah and all of Jerusalem discovered that. The historical reference to the nations raging and falling depict the ravages of the Assyrian conquest, but because Judah trusted in the Lord, his timely intervention of the plague was performed.

Right now the tempest is raging. The billows are high. But we never walk alone. Yes! When we know that God is by our side, we can confidently expect him to intervene and do what we most need in our trouble. God is constantly at work preparing people, arranging circumstances, changing situations to bring a resolution to the trouble we face.

3) *God gives us peace on the inside.* The psalmist reviewed the awesome way the Lord intervened for Judah.

Come, behold the works of the LORD;
see what desolations he has brought on the earth.
He makes wars cease to the end of the earth;
he breaks the bow, and shatters the spear;
he burns the shields with fire (verses 8–9).

The psalmist reviews. We, too, need to review what the Lord has already done for us. Then suddenly God speaks and our souls tremble.

"Be still, and know that I am God!
I am exalted among the nations,
I am exalted in the earth" (verse 10).

Be still and know God is able. Be still and know God is sovereign. Be still and know our extremity is God's opportunity. Be still and know that earth has no sorrow that heaven cannot heal.

Why Are There So Many Crosses?

Don E. Gibson

Rev. Don Gibson *is pastor of Memorial Christian Church in Oklahoma City, Oklahoma. He is active in neighborhood ecumenical ministries that focus on serving the community.*

Matthew 23:1–12

After grieving with those who have suffered the death of loved ones, we look at the devastation of the Federal Building in disbelief. Almost everyone has asked the twin questions: Who did this? Who planned, planted, and detonated the bomb that killed little children and innocent adults? The second question is: Why? Why would anyone do such a horrible and evil deed?

Yes, we have a suspect in prison. Speculations as to why he bombed the Federal Building are pouring forth. This morning I think it is important that we as Christians ask the right questions and be open to search for answers that are deeper than the TV commentators usually pursue. Let us turn the question,

"How could anyone do such a terrible thing?" into a religious question: *Why must there be so many crosses?*

We know more about the roots of violence than we often are willing to admit. I believe that the scripture reading of the morning provides a good beginning point for understanding why someone bombed the Federal Building. This passage does not give us a clue as to why the target was the Federal Building, but it provides a clue for understanding the roots of violence.

> "They do all their deeds to be seen by others.... They love to have the place of honor at banquets and the best seats in the synagogues, and to be greeted with respect in the marketplaces, and to have people call them rabbi" (Matthew 23:5a, 6).

In this passage Jesus is talking about what is in the hearts of the Pharisees. But I think this description applies to any and all of us. How often is our behavior calculated to impress other people? Sure, I like to be seated at the head table and be treated with honor. You know I desire to be treated with respect. Of course I want people to listen to my ideas and look upon me as one who knows what I'm talking about—an expert in my field. And what is my field? Well, it just so happens that I'm an authority on any subject on which you have a question. When Jesus was describing the desires and inner workings in the minds and hearts of the Pharisees, he was talking about a lot of us, if not all of us: a desire to be popular, to impress other people, to be treated with respect, to be looked upon as an authority—universal desires!

That's only part of the picture. The universal desires of the human heart are also combined with messages from our society. What are some of the dominant messages we are taught from infancy? Here are a few of the dominant messages:

"Nobody tells me what to do!" We hear this attitude at least as early as kindergarten. It sounds kind of cute and we may laugh it off when a child tells the teacher: "You're not my mother! I don't have to do what you say!" But all too soon the child doesn't even feel any obligation to listen to Mother.

Here are two more popular attitudes that become deeply ingrained at a fairly young age: "**Nobody pushes me around!**" and "**I'll do as I damn well please!**" These attitudes combine and result in what I call a sense of *individual sovereignty*. When we mix our desires for attention, recognition, honor, respect, with our attitudes of individual sovereignty, what do we get? What we get is a lot of people whose egos demand that they *dominate, control,* and *get their own way*. What we get are people who like to *push other people around* and think that being mean and ugly to others is normal and natural.

Believe me, these desires and attitudes are expressed at a very early age. They are expressed in the child throwing a temper tantrum in order to get attention or to get what she wants. These characteristics appear in a child who becomes the playground bully. Worse yet, these characteristics are revealed in the parent who proudly sticks the bumper sticker on the family car that says, "MY KID BEAT UP YOUR HONOR STUDENT!" Then we wonder why there are so many crosses in the world!

Crosses are there because we teach children to get their way by temper tantrums, bullying, and violence! There are so many crosses because, by example, adults teach that the goal in life is to get our own way *and the means by which we get our way don't matter!* Thus, we justify the use of a variety of forms of violence, intimidation, sarcasm, name calling, and finally terrorism. We see these expressions of violence in personal relationships in the home, workplace, marketplace and even in the church.

I know that it sounds like an exaggeration to say that there is a relationship between the infant who throws himself or herself on the floor, kicking and screaming in a temper tantrum, and the bombing of the Federal Building. But there is a continuum of behavior by people who will do anything to get their way. Why are there so many crosses? Because there are people who are willing to intimidate and use violence to get their way. Because there are people who will use violence to push others around as a way of building their egos. Because there are people who think they are superior and have a right to use violence against others who are inferior.

When we feel that we have been treated with disrespect, we get our feelings hurt; when we have not been asked to sit at the head of the banquet table, we get our feelings hurt. People with hurt feelings may become persons with a desire for revenge and retaliation. When our ideas are ignored, when our views are laughed at, we feel put down. People who are put down may develop a desire for retaliation and revenge. When someone steps on our toes by accident, we expect them to apologize. But when people step on our toes on purpose, we feel they deserve to be punished—and we feel we have the right to punish them.

Do you see how many situations occur that provide us with good reasons to engage in what we consider to be *justified violence*? Then we wonder why there are so many crosses!

We live in a society—indeed, in a world—in which there are literally millions of people walking around feeling that they have a right for retaliation, revenge, and violence. Then we wonder why there are so many crosses!

One news report on the bombing reported on the growing number of units in various states called citizen's militias. One commander of a state militia group explained that such things as the bombing the Federal Building happen because there are many citizens convinced that government is evil and sinister. He said, and I quote: "We [militia operations] must be ready to balance the scales of justice, which requires engaging in the practice of an eye for an eye and a tooth for a tooth." The worst part of his speech was that he defined his group and his beliefs as part of what he defined as a "Christian militia."

Friends, those two words, *Christian* and *militia*, are a contradiction. Those two words are opposites. And we as Christians must strongly voice our objection to people who seek to justify their hatred, fear, and violence under the banner of being Christian!

We should be outraged when Jesus is held up as a teacher of an eye for an eye or a tooth for a tooth. We must not permit his name to be used to justify retaliation and revenge and violence. Our struggle as Christians is to find ways to oppose evil without ourselves becoming evil. It requires our most creative thought and practice to find ways to oppose violence without becoming violent.

Why are there so many crosses? Why was Jesus crucified? Because he would not become like his enemies. Jesus would not become like his enemies, even to save his own life. He chose to die rather than to return evil with evil, rather than return violence with violence. Listen to the way 1 Peter describes Jesus:

> For to this you have been called, because Christ also suffered for you, leaving you an example, so that you should follow in his steps. "He committed no sin, and no deceit was found in his mouth." When he was abused, he did not return abuse; when he suffered, he did not threaten; but he entrusted himself to the one who judges justly (1 Peter 2:21–23).

The enemies of Jesus threw everything in their arsenal of weapons at him: taunts, tricks, false charges, trumped-up trial, buy-off of one of his followers, plots, a crown of thorns, a sword in the side and nails in his hands and feet. Yes, he felt abandoned. "My God, why have you forsaken me!" But he would not return violence against violence. He would not become like his enemies.

Friends, I have the same feelings that many of you have: grief, anger, revenge, retaliation. That same feeling Jesus expressed. "My God, why? Why have you forsaken us?" But I struggle and ask you to struggle. "For to this you have been called, because Christ also suffered for you, leaving you an example, so that you should follow in his steps." Those steps are the steps of one who would not become like his enemies.

Let us pray:

God, help us to oppose evil without becoming evil!
God, help us oppose violence without becoming violent!
Amen!

Who Is the Owner of the Heartland of America?

Dr. J. N. Ahmad

Dr. Ahmad *is imam of Iqraa Amerika and delivers a Muslim response to the bombing. He is also a physician at the Shawnee Indian Health Clinic. He is a member of the steering committee of the Interfaith Disaster Recovery of Greater Oklahoma City, which is coordinating the long-term recovery needs of the entire community.*

On the momentous day of April 19, 1995, a terrorist nightmare bombing struck the heart of Oklahoma City, which is in the heart of Oklahoma, which is in the heart of America. The physical shock waves produced subsequent psychological shock waves that have reached human hearts throughout our nation and the world.

The people of America and the world community will never be the same again. For if the vital heart of our beloved nation is a vulnerable prey to the beastly fangs of terrorist attack, then all people are at risk.

It has been said that this disaster is unfathomable and beyond human comprehension. However, I humbly submit to you that as people of faith we must begin unceasingly to seek, knock, and ask until the door of hidden wisdom and understanding of the meaning of this event is opened unto us. The terrorized hearts of our children, as well as our hearts, are in crying need of answers that make sense.

Although it may take the people of faith many years of praying and probing to obtain meaningful answers, our journey toward spiritual insights into the bombing of the Alfred Paul Murrah Federal Building must be treated with the same reverence as a religious pilgrimage. I believe that we owe this respect for spiritual pilgrimage to the deceased victims, the living victims, ourselves, our human family, and our Universal Creator.

In fact, as I read in the *Daily Oklahoman* of National Guardsman Sgt. Medina's effort to build a sacred shrine near the site of the Murrah Building, the sacred places in Medina, Mecca, and Jerusalem were brought to mind. These three cities contain areas that are held as sacred to peoples of Al-Islam, or the Islamic faith. Vital centers in Jerusalem are holy to Judaism, Christianity, and Al-Islam.

It is noteworthy that this event occurred during the month of April, at a time that was very special for humanity's Jewish, Christian, and Muslim peoples. It is not often that both the Jewish Passover as well as the events of Easter occur so close in time.

In addition, hundreds of thousands of peoples of the Islamic faith were preparing in April for the annual pilgrimage to Mecca that began the first of May. In fact, for the first time in many years the beginning of the month of May corresponded with the onset of the month of the pilgrimage—called the Hajj.

As I reflected on the journey of Muslims to the spiritual place of devotion that is at the heart of the Islamic faith, it was inviting to compare the two heartlands—the heartland of America and the spiritual heartland in Mecca.

National Guardsman Sgt. Medina followed his natural humanitarian impulse to build a simple shrine. The shrine was designed to provide a protective shelter from unpredictable harshness in conditions of weather. He could not bear the thought of the precious memorial site being exposed to the whims of unpredictable rain and unruly weather. He was quoted as saying that this site in the heartland of America was "sacred."

As a Muslim member of the Islamic faith, I was deeply touched by the words and charitable deeds of Sgt. Medina (with the help of his wife and concerned friends). Just as Sgt. Medina experienced the natural feelings of the personal sanctity and sacredness of this memorial site in the heartland of America, the hearts of pilgrims in Mecca and Medina were experiencing a similar reverent respect.

In Mecca the precious territory that represents the symbolic spiritual heartland of Al-Islam is called the Ka'bah, or the House of God. Today's Ka'bah is at the site of the original ancient House that was built by Prophet Abraham. Prophet Abraham is a spiritual father who is a sign of the unity of the peoples of Judaic, Christian, and Islamic beliefs long before the surface labels identified us as separate communities of people. For each of these three communities of faith, Abraham is our father.

The temporary period for the guarding and securing of the Murrah Building by National Guardsmen provides an interesting contrast with the daily year-round guarding of the symbolic sacred territory of God's Building. Muslims call God, the Creator, Allah. The territory that symbolizes God's Building in God's heartland is viewed as a sacred and inviolable place by Muslims.

There is a beloved stone that is at the corner of the House of God. This precious stone is said to have descended from the heavenly realm of God, down to earth within reach of mortal humanity. The House of God has been built by men with brick, or blocks of stony clay. Through Prophet Abraham, humanity was given both a universal pattern for building, as well as a universal heavenly stone, at the corner and foundation of God's Building.

The House of God-given life is to be built around and upon the universal stone in accord with the pattern molded by God. The Arabic root word for *ka'bah* includes words that identify the chest, or house of the heart, or the heartland that is within us.

Like embryonic human developments in the womb of our mothers, we are free to grow upon the natural pattern that has been established by God. This natural design is preserved in the genetic seed language that is inherited through generations over time. The human embryo has the natural freedom that is limited to express itself in accord with the inherited plan of God. If the developmental building of human life in the womb deviates significantly from the universal pattern for growth, spontaneous miscarriage is the most common result.

The Ka'bah, or the House of God, has been called a symbol of the region of the unseen spiritual heart. In fact, the Arabic root word for house is *bayt*. This root word refers to the place where we spend the night. During each night of sleep, human hearts experience the world of the unseen hidden life of the heart.

Many of the same fears that we experienced in our hearts as children continue to haunt the unseen spiritual mind of the human being. The field of mental health calls the vital unseen spiritual mind the subconscious or unconscious mind. The terror of nightmares, anxiety-filled flashbacks, overwhelming panic attacks, and post-traumatic stress disorder provide clear lasting evidence of the devastating blast that has violated the hidden spiritual heartland of the victims of this terrorist bombing.

The mental reality of the unseen psychological shock waves that were produced by the physical terrorist bombing of the Murrah Building should never be forgotten. The unseen terrorist assault upon the hidden spiritual identity of the heartland within us must be studied with religious devotion.

The American society has been brought face-to-face with the ancient reality of the paralyzing terror that can explode in the spiritual heartland of the human soul. Let us ever be mindful of the need to remove from our thinking the slabs of concrete, physical views of the human being's real and universal identity. Buried beneath the fragmented concrete slabs of the Murrah Building is the real identity of two lives that are precious to Jews, Christians, and Muslims: Virgin-ia and Christ-i.

The spiritual heartland can be compared to a virgin womb for building human developments upon the one and only foundation that has been established by God. Within a physical womb that is filled with acquired contagious social diseases, developing life is at high risk to become infected and aborted. Similarly, the failure to guard the virginity of the spiritual subconscious womb from contagious social diseases threatens to abort the Christlike development within the heartland.

It is said in the life teachings of Prophet Muhammad that the Dajjal, or antichrist, will not be able to enter and capture the cities of Mecca and Medina. Muslims believe in the vigilant guardianship over the sacred centers that represent the spiritual heartland. Clearly, if antichrist man-made social diseases are not to abort within us the saving power of the Christlike building upon the one and only foundation created by God, the national guardianship of the virginity of God's heartland must become a major issue in human societies throughout the world.

Baha'i Reflections

Khalil Dana

Mr. Dana is a layperson who offers a Baha'i response to the bombing. A tireless volunteer, he is chairman of the Interfaith Disaster Recovery of Greater Oklahoma City.

"Whatever hath befallen you, hath been for the sake of God. This is the truth, and in this there is no doubt. You should, therefore, leave all your affairs in His hands, place your trust in Him, and rely upon Him. He will assuredly not forsake you. In this, likewise, there is no doubt. No father will surrender his sons to devouring beasts; no shepherd will leave his flock to ravening wolves. He will most certainly do his utmost to protect his own.

"If, however, for a few days, in compliance with God's all-encompassing wisdom, outward affairs should run their course contrary to one's cherished desire, this is of no consequence and should not matter."

Whatever suffering and turmoil the years immediately ahead may hold, however dark the immediate circumstances, the Baha'i community believes that humanity can confront this supreme trial with confidence in its ultimate outcome. The convulsive changes toward which humanity is being ever more rapidly impelled will serve to release the "potentialities inherent in the station of man" and reveal "the full measure of his destiny on earth, the innate excellence of his reality."

The causes of conflict and war must be eliminated. Banning weapons, prohibiting the use of poison gases, or outlawing germ warfare will not remove the root causes of war and conflict. However important such practical measures obviously are as elements of the peace process, they are in themselves too superficial to exert enduring influence. Peoples are ingenious enough to invent yet other forms of warfare, and to use food, raw materials, finance, industrial power, ideology, and terrorism to subvert one another in an endless quest for supremacy and dominion.

Baha'u'llah tells us that religion itself is the "greatest of all means for the establishment of order in the world and for the peaceful contentment of all that dwell therein. Should the lamp of religion be obscured, chaos and confusion will ensue, and the lights of fairness, of justice, of tranquillity and peace cease to shine."

The power of religion unites the hearts of men and women, one heart at a time, which will ultimately bring peace and unity. This peaceful world we seek "can be founded only on an unshakable consciousness of the oneness of mankind, a spiritual truth which all the human sciences confirm. Anthropology, physiology, psychology, recognize only one human species, albeit infinitely varied in the secondary aspects of life. Recognition of this truth requires abandonment of prejudice—prejudice of every kind—race, class, color, creed, nation, sex, degree of material civilization, everything which enables people to consider themselves superior to others.

"The well-being of mankind, its peace and security, are unattainable, unless and until its unity is firmly established.

"The gift of God to this enlightened age is the knowledge of the oneness of mankind and of the fundamental oneness of religion. War shall cease between the nations, and by the will of God the Most Great Peace shall come; the world will be seen as a new world, and all men will live as brothers."

Quotations are excerpts from Baha'i Writings.

Words, Words, Words: an Enduring Gift

Don H. Alexander

Within hours of the bombing, Don Alexander *offered the entire facilities of First Christian Church as a safe haven for families to wait for news of their loved ones. It was designated the Family Assistance Center, and for the next three weeks, it remained open twenty-four hours a day, teeming with hundreds of people—Red Cross, Salvation Army, National Guard, volunteer chaplains, mental health workers, media representatives, and volunteers of all kinds. This sermon was delivered on April 30, 1995.*

Genesis 1:1–5; John 1:1–5

Words, words, words. Have you ever heard so many words as in this last week? In the book of Genesis, God spoke the world...no, that's not quite what it says...God spoke the *shape* of the world into being. The world already existed when God began to create, but it was a disordered mess—*tohu va bohu* in Hebrew. And I like that translation that reads, "In the beginning, when God began to create..." because it reminds us that creation still goes on and, once in a while, in a horrific, awful way, the *tohu va bohu*, the disordered mess, can break out again in our midst, and we are tempted to be defined by it. Then out of hearts of lovingkindness comes a response that says, "No!

That is not who God made us to be. We will not be defined by acts of evil, darkness, insanity, and chaos!"

Words...I began our announcements this morning by speaking "thank yous," by affirming you and this facility, by affirming the media, by affirming those who work on our behalf, by speaking our sympathy to those families who have been so deeply affected. I used words. Words are not adequate, but they are what we have. And even though they are not adequate, we have our biblical witness that they are powerful. Even as God spoke shape for the world into being, so we have spoken shape to our existence in this past week and a half.

We are different now, aren't we? We have discovered a capacity within ourselves, within our community and, yes, within our world that we had perhaps forgotten was there. We continue to seek to understand and interpret it. And I don't know any other way but to use words.

I have been interviewed dozens of times these last eleven days and I have felt that it was my responsibility to seek the words to shape the interpretation of what we are experiencing. We cannot change what has happened, but how we respond to what has happened can work an eternal change in us.

A reporter from Great Britain called me three times yesterday morning. Finally, at 11:30 a.m., the call came to talk with Cullen, who was going to be interviewing me on their 5:30 a.m. broadcast. It was live—11:30 a.m. here, but 5:30 p.m. there. And Cullen asked, "Will the goodness grow thin? I mean, will you wear down emotionally? Will you lose your focus?"

Yes, I answered, to some degree that will happen. We are already feeling emotionally drained. But there has been established a reservoir, a new sense of self, a new quality of response. Did you hear what one reporter called it? "The Oklahoma standard." That's wonderful! I wonder if the time will ever come when we'll tire of living up to "The Oklahoma standard"? Oh, I hope not! I hope that when we are tempted to do that, we will say, "No, no." We've redefined who we are, as individuals, as a community, as Christians, as people in community with people of other faiths. We've redefined who we are. We cannot change what has happened, but how we respond and continue to respond can work an eternal change in us.

This is a teachable moment. And it is a deeply theological moment, because everything we say is under a microscope. It's going to be magnified. Everything we say is going to be an expression of our deepest sense of what God is like. And if we speak shallow words, if we're glib and too quick in our response, we may give a glib and shallow reflection of the God whom we seek to serve. So we must be careful to be sure there's heart in our words, because there is, indeed, heart in our God. In fact, this teachable moment is a long moment. We don't know how long, but I'm convinced that with our words we will be interpreting what has happened and our response to it. And what has happened these last eleven days will affect our theology, our response to life from now on.

There are some things in this teachable, theological moment that we must not say. Well, I've already heard them said, and yet, somehow, we must call ourselves to attention and understand that some of these things—which have been said with deep feeling and emotion, and perhaps have been comforting to those who said them—shouldn't have been said, at least not in the way they were said.

It will not have the same impact, the same effect on our mental and emotional health, if we wait too long to nuance our language, to understand the implications of what we are saying. So I have brought my script. If you feel like the preacher has jumped on you with both feet, please remember that this preacher has also spoken words that he wishes he hadn't said.

Here are some phrases I have heard this past week. Let's see if we can NOT use them, NOT speak them. A woman called from Lawton to express her care and concern. And then, in frustration, she said, "Well, we just have to know that somehow everything fits in God's plan." This is not what Romans 8 says. I don't think God's plan is finished yet. I think we're in the process of helping God write that plan. When chaos erupts, that is not what God wants; that's not in God's plan. The explosion at 9:02 a.m. on April 19, 1995, at the Murrah Building doesn't fit into God's plan. God's heart broke that morning, just as ours did. I believe we must speak that word clearly, just now, so we aren't guilty of fuzzy thinking in the weeks and months and years and lives to come.

Expressing how deeply grateful he and his family were, a man said to me, "We got our miracle." Their son, who was in the building, was not killed, not even injured. That is a wonderful thing. And if you use the word *miracle* to describe an unusually marvelous event, then that was a miracle. But if you use the popular understanding of the word *miracle* as a supernatural act, God's intervention, then you are saying God acted capriciously—saving some, killing others. So, be careful how you use the word *miracle*, because we worship a God who is neither fickle nor capricious. We can't say all that God is. But being created in the image of God, we can say some things God is not. God is not capricious. God is lovingkindness. There were no choices made by God in this event. The explosion was an act of evil. To choose for some people to survive while innocent children were killed is not what God is like.

One of our political leaders said, "If God is good, they will be found alive." I know the man who spoke those words meant well. But we must examine our words and take care how we speak. That statement would say to some, when so many people were not found alive, that God is not good. Wrong words, because they say the wrong thing about God.

I want to be careful because I am about to quote something that has touched people's lives. There is a poem that has been often quoted on one of the network channels here in Oklahoma City, and they have meant well by it. It's entitled "To All Parents," by Edgar A. Guest—verses 1, 2 and 6. Sometimes words that drip with sentiment can comfort us, but I believe they are short-term comforts. If those words use phrases like "It may be six or seven years, or twenty-two or three, but will you, till I call him back, take care of him for me?" they suggest that God is the active instrument in taking our children away from us.

The sixth verse reads: "Will you give him all your love, nor think the labor vain, nor hate me when I come to call to take him back again?" God does not manipulate or directly control human events. My deep conviction is that God was not allowed into the hearts of the perpetrators of this awful act. They had shut God out—because if God had been there, it would not have happened.

Do your daily choices matter? Only if God has released us in this creative act—this process of creation—only if God has released us into freedom—where we make real choices and real decisions and our "yes" means "yes" and our "no" means "no." And our prejudices hurt somebody and our lovingkindness matters. See how careful we must be with our words?

We'll continue to wrestle with this, won't we? Because the preacher said this morning that, as he understands God, God does not manipulatively or directly control human events. "How could God allow this to happen?" is an inappropriate question to ask because if you ask the question that way it assumes that God could have stopped it from happening.

I have the image in my mind of a little child playing in the front yard. An evil person drives down the street of that neighborhood and pulls over to the curb, opens the door, gets out and goes to the child that's playing, and suddenly yanks the child up and runs to his vehicle and speeds away. That child has been taken. Is that what God is like? Then I have another image, an image of mom and dad, or maybe it's grandmom and granddad or grammy and poppy, who drive up. The child is playing in the yard. The car doors are opened, the child looks up and sees those persons who represent security, safety, lovingkindness—and that child turns from his or her playing and runs pell-mell, full force into the arms of receiving love. So when I quote the text in John 14—"Do not let your hearts be troubled. Believe in God, believe also in me. In my Father's house are many dwelling places. If it were not so, would I have told you that I go to prepare a place for you? And if I go…, I will come again and will take you to myself"—I sense that is what God is like.

Everything we say about God is metaphorical—let's put that right up front. Otherwise, if we were saying that our words were God, it would be idolatrous, but we need to shape our understanding of what God is like. I see God in images of lovingkindness. I see God in images that call light out of darkness, order out of chaos. What are some of your favorite images? Hold onto them, treasure them, say to those you love, "This is what God is like."

We sang one of them this morning for our opening hymn, didn't we? "A Mighty Fortress is our God, a bulwark never failing." I don't believe I have ever conducted a funeral service that I did not say, "The Lord is my shepherd." We need that in life services as well, don't we? The Lord is our shepherd, the one who guards, holds, and seeks us when we are lost.

We live in a marvelous tradition of faith, a tradition that helps us span the distance between physical and spiritual, between this life and what is beyond this life. We have images of lovingkindness, luring us, drawing us on. Listen to these words from Paul in 2 Corinthians, the fourth chapter: "So we do not lose heart. Even though our outer nature is wasting away, our inner nature is being renewed day by day. For…we look not at what can be seen but at what cannot be seen; for what can be seen is temporary, but what cannot be seen is eternal. For we know that if the earthly tent we live in is destroyed, we have a building from God, a house not made with hands, eternal in the heavens."

Words, words, words. Treat them gently, carefully. They are an enduring gift. Amen.

Epilogue

David P. Polk

The site that had been the Alfred P. Murrah Federal Building has now been imploded into a pile of rubble. The final bodies have been recovered. Exhausted rescue workers have all gone home. But the scars remain—on the cityscape of America's heartland and in the hearts of resilient Oklahomans.

This collection of sermons, addresses, and prayers arose from the crucible of devastation in the hours and days following the April 19 bombing. The voices on these pages come from men and women who, for the most part, were intensely involved in disaster recovery activities from Wednesday through Saturday of that week and barely had time to retreat into their studies to ponder the task of bringing God's word in a healing, empowering way to a people in tumult and grief. Given the difficult circumstances, the eloquence of their preaching is remarkable.

Answers to the senseless shattering of lives do not come easy for compassionate people of faith. Searing questions are raised unflinchingly. What shines through is the tenacious conviction that God's loving intentions toward us are not defeated by the forces of rampant destruction. Evil and death do not have the last word. The last word belongs to the One whose caring face is always turned toward us—no matter what the adversity each of us may encounter.